FIRE ME I BEG YOU

QUIT YOUR MISERABLE JOB (WITHOUT RISKING IT ALL)

ROBBIE ABED

FMIBY

CONTENTS

Fire Me I Beg You   v
Foreword   ix
Preface   xiii
Introduction   xv

SECTION ONE: MAKING A DECISION

1. The Honest Truth About Quitting   3
2. Why You Should Quit Your Job   6
3. Question-And-Answer Time   11

SECTION TWO - SURVIVAL MODE

4. Broke Trip To Aldi   17
5. Intro To Survival Mode   23
6. Financials 101   25
7. Time Management 101   32
8. Psychology 101   43
9. Offline Professional Networking 101   50
10. Online Networking 101   69

SECTION THREE: THE TRADITIONAL ROUTE

11. Your Path May Vary   81
12. Replace Your Awful Job With A Better One 84

13. Everything You Need To Know About Finding A Job   93

14. How To Nail Any Interview   98

15. The Slimy, Greedy, Utterly Necessary Game of Salary Negotiation   110

SECTION FOUR: THE NON-TRADITIONAL ROUTE

16. Are You A Failure If You Need To Work A 9-5?   121

17. 7 Week Entrepreneurship Plan   127

SECTION FIVE: THE QUITTING PLAYBOOK

18. Ready, Set, Quit   145

19. The Famous Resignation Letter   150

20. Whatever Decision You Make, It Will Be Wrong   160

APPENDIX

How To Answer The Most Common Interview Questions   167

Case Studies   181

Acknowledgments   205

But Wait — There's More!   207

FIRE ME I BEG YOU

Quit Your Miserable Job (Without Risking It All)

Robbie Abed

DEDICATION

To my wife: This book wouldn't be possible without you. Thank you for putting up with me and supporting me all of these years. I need the support more than you think.

To my daughter, Danya: At the time of this writing, you are three years old. You are smart, funny and you know how to get what you want. You also hate putting on your jacket in the winter. I fight with you every morning before school because you refuse to put on your jacket or your boots. I don't think you'll last in Chicago long.

To my unborn daughter: You are due to be born any day now. We don't know what we're going to name you. Maybe Sophia. Maybe Zayna. Maybe Tesneem. The only advice I have for you is to work hard and be yourself. Also, I have a feeling that your big sister Danya is going to bully you around when you get older. Stand up to her. But, just know she'll always support you.

To my father: I will always miss you. I definitely got my sick sense of humor from you.

To my mother: You're the hardest-working person I know. Thank you for always supporting me and helping me become the person I am today.

To my brother and sister: One of these days, you both will figure out what I do for a living. Thank you for your continued support.

To everyone else: I always dreamed of dedicating a book to my haters, but to be honest, I haven't had many haters in my writing career. Except this one guy who left me one of the nastiest comments on a blog post I've ever seen. This book is for you buddy. I hope you find your peace.

FOREWORD

JAMES ALTUCHER

Robbie Abed wanted to have coffee with me in 2011. Then in 2012, and 2013, and 2014. I kept saying no.

Robbie told me he has 250 coffee meetings a year.

So in one way of thinking about it, I'm one in 250. And over a period of four years, I'm one in a thousand. So, not so special.

I don't usually meet new people for coffee. I like to sit in my room and read, and write, and deal with business stuff. A few months ago I was on a three-week vacation to Thailand one block from the beach and it took me two weeks to get to the beach.

Robbie wrote to me and said, "I'll even come to where you are." I live 80 miles north of NYC. I figured he was bluffing.

So I said, "ok, but I only have 15 minutes." Who is going to drive 1.5 hours to have coffee with me for 15 minutes and then drive 1.5 hours back to the city?

He said, "ok." And I said, "ok, meet me at 12:15." And I gave him the address, "but I might be late," because I had a podcast that started at 11.

When my podcast was over, he was there. I didn't want to have coffee. So I said, "come back to my house and let's do a podcast." He came back with me and I did an 'Ask Altucher' podcast with him, "Why do you have 250 coffee meetings a year?"

He described that he was in a bad job situation several years ago and had no network at all.

He was scared. He wanted to go on his own but he was afraid to go broke.

He wanted to figure out how to make connections. So he joined a networking group and started having coffee with everyone in the group and asking them, "how can I help you? Who can I introduce to you?"

This is a great question. About 50% of people consider themselves too shy to introduce themselves to other people. Maybe the real number is even higher. I consider myself a shy person. In a party I hide and just like to watch people.

For Robbie, if someone said, "I want to meet X." he would then try to have coffee with X, he'd mention that the other person wants to meet X and why. If X was agreeable, he'd make the introduction.

I call this "permission networking." If you just introduce two people without their permission then you just contributed to ruining their lives.

You outsourced the question of "Why should these two people meet" to them instead of solving the problem yourself.

Many people don't want to figure out why they should meet someone. They are already busy enough.

Hence, everyone will hate you, the guy in the middle that gave them more work to do.

Robbie described all the ways he benefited from these coffee meetings.

Sometimes he would and sometimes he wouldn't. Some people would pay him and some would ignore him. But bit by bit, having 250 coffees a year allowed him to build a successful marketing business.

THE 250 COFFEES A YEAR TECHNIQUE:

- Join a networking group, or have some other excuse to call people and tell them how you could potentially help them if they had a cup of coffee with you.
- Try to learn at least one thing from them in the coffee meeting.
- Research them in advance so you might be able to guess what their needs are.
- Focus on the other person's needs. "How can I help you?"
- Do this 250 times a year.
- Follow through. Be that guy.
- Stay out of the way and have no expectations.

Before Robbie left my house he described someone who created an interesting model in the restaurant business. "Whoa," I said, "that's pretty cool."

It made me think, "this person would be interesting for my podcast. What an innovative way to do restaurants."

Within 40 minutes, Robbie had reached out to the person, got his permission, and then sent an intro to the two of us.

I looked back through my emails. I saw that Robbie wrote me in January 2011. He said, "Thank you for everything you've done for me," even though I hadn't done anything for him.

I'm not even sure I responded to that one.

Well Robbie, thank you for everything you've done for me.

Fire Me I Beg You is a book about how to succeed when real life gets in the way. I think you'll enjoy it.

I'm going to keep this preface short.

There is only one reason you are reading this book.

You want to quit your job, but you can't.

There are two main reasons why you haven't quit yet.

1. Financial reasons
2. Fear of the unknown

The crazy part is that you're going to have to plunge into the unknown eventually.

What do I mean by that?

You're playing a game of musical chairs, and it's just a matter of time until you have no chair to sit on. The music is going to stop any second now, and there isn't a damn thing you can do about it.

Few jobs *won't* be affected by the rise of automation. And I'm not talking about a century from now—I'm talking about 10, 15, and

20 years from now. According to the World Economic Forum, "65% of children entering primary school today will ultimately end up working in completely new job types that don't yet exist."As our machines get smarter, robots, cognitive machines, and the simple software on your computer will render old jobs obsolete. In other words, there is no such thing as job security.

Look at this this way: Hating your job might be the best thing that could've happened to you. It's a kick in the pants to learn survival skills for the coming jobpocalypse.

The goal of this book is twofold: to help you get out before the music stops, and to teach you skills to find a job you love. Not just once, but anytime, anywhere, in any economic climate, with almost any salary goal.

You didn't hear that wrong.

My boss set up an emergency meeting in her office. The title of the calendar invite was "catch up." It was one of those vague meeting titles that meant one of two things:

1) She wanted to catch up, or...

2) She was going to fire me.

The meeting was sent at 2:00 a.m. and it was for 6 hours later at 8:00 a.m. The moment I got the email, my mind started going wild.

What in the world does she want to talk about?

There was no description in the email; she surely is going to lay me off. She never sends emails this late at night. The company isn't doing that well. This has to be it. I'm toast.

In every situation, I ask myself two questions:

- What do I want the outcome of this situation to be?

- What do I secretly want the outcome of this situation to be?

My first, and less honest answer was that I really hoped she just wanted to catch up on my to-do list. I had a family to feed and nothing really lined up job-wise. I couldn't afford to be laid off right then. It was Christmas time, so nobody was hiring. *Please just let this be a follow-up meeting to discuss future goals,* I thought.

What do I secretly want the outcome of this situation to be?

Fire me. I beg you. End my misery right now. This isn't the right job for me. I don't want to be doing this right now.

This is not what I signed up for. Every day I come to this job I lose a part of my soul. I have been coming to work late for the past two months now. Can't you see that I just don't care anymore?

Can't you recognize that? I'm not meant for the corporate life anymore. I want to create something meaningful. I want to create something that others are going to use. I want to do the things that I'm good at. For the love of everything almighty. Fire me. Please.

I recalled an incident from a few months prior. I'd heard the words "Sir, what are you doing?" from behind me.

"I... I'm just getting a pen."

"This supply cabinet is for employees of this group only. Are you part of this group?"

"I... I'm sorry. I thought this cabinet was for everyone within the company?"

"Well, it's not. The nerve of some people. Put that down please."

I walked away feeling like a criminal and embarrassed. Two hours later I was laughing to myself and thinking, "Wow. What a miserable person that lady was."

What does being miserable feel like? There is being unhappy and unsatisfied at work, and then there is complete misery. Here's how you know if you're miserable:

- You take a deep breath each morning before checking your email for the first time.
- When people ask how you're doing, you say, "I'M DOING GREAT," when in reality you are one snide comment away from a mental breakdown.
- When your boss is talking to you, you're making eye contact, but inside you're screaming so loudly that you're almost positive she can hear you.
- When you go home, you replay different work interactions a million times in your head, saying all of all the things you wish you could have said.

It wasn't just the office culture—it was the work/life balance.

I was setting myself on fire to keep someone else warm. I did whatever it took to finish a deliverable. I worked days, nights, weekends, holidays, family events, summer days, snow days, football games, leap days, St. Patrick's Days, BBQs and birthdays. I was a machine.

Here's the kicker. No one ever demanded that I worked this much. I did it on my own. I set myself on fire to exceed the expectations of my manager and colleagues.

Later, I'd learn that it wasn't my boss' job to tell me that I was working too much. Let me make this a little bit more real for you. Your boss won't tell you that you're working too much.

You know what, I'm going to go deeper on this one, because I don't think you understand: Your boss will let you continue to overwork yourself without any regard to how it affects your personal life. It's not their job to manage your personal life. That's your job.

Back to my boss and our 8:00 a.m. meeting: She just wanted to catch up.

It was a bittersweet feeling, but in the end I realized that I needed do what I secretly wanted to do all along. One month later I quit. If she wasn't going to end my secret misery, then I was.

SECTION ONE: MAKING A DECISION

CHAPTER ONE

THE HONEST TRUTH ABOUT QUITTING

QUITTING MY JOB FORCED ME TO BECOME DESPERATE. IT forced a quarter-life crisis.

At 31, I quit my job and went out utterly and completely on my own. I had no 9–5 job. No one to report to. I started from a blank slate.

I wrote 140 blog articles the year I quit, hoping to both grow my network and to perhaps help someone with the cache of business knowledge I'd amassed. When I quit, I had no choice but to succeed. It was by far the most challenging year of my life.

I quit without anything lined up. I jumped right into the deep end without a life jacket. (The point of this book, by the way, is to chart a smoother course to a new job, so you won't have to go through the harrowing experience I did.)

What happens when you get desperate? You do desperate things.

- I took 250 coffee meetings in 400 days.
- I went to every networking event imaginable.

- I explored different career paths. I think I changed my career at least 4 times that year.
- I created things that nobody wanted.
- I read every business book possible.
- I didn't really know what I wanted to do with my life, and most importantly I didn't know where my next paycheck would be coming from.

Here's what's the most interesting. **Quitting my job made me a better person.** If I hadn't, I wouldn't be where I am today.

Quitting is actually a euphemism. It's a nice way to say, "You'll probably go through depression, question every life decision you've ever made, make some friends, definitely a few more enemies, but don't worry, you'll get it over it and it will be the best experience you'll ever have."

The reason that quitting my job made me a better person is because I not only have 100% clarity on what I want to do with my life, I have clarity on what I *don't* want to do with my life. Of course, during the dip, I was the most confused I've ever been, but once I got out of it, it changed my entire perspective.

Ask any entrepreneur about the lowest point of their career and they'll talk about it as if they're a Vietnam War veteran reminiscing about war stories. And they will also tell you that their personal low point was one of the most rewarding experiences of their lives. One they'll never regret embarking on.

Quitting was an incredibly rewarding experience for me.

If I hadn't quit my job, I would have never learned how to write. I would have never learned digital marketing. My relationships would be weak, untested, and one-dimensional. I wouldn't have made the earth-shattering realization that others actually wanted to hear what I have to say.

And most importantly, quitting taught me that I could go from zero dollars in my bank account, with no safety net, to financial stability in a short time frame.

I not only learned how to survive, I also learned how to thrive without the support of a full-time job.

CHAPTER TWO

WHY YOU SHOULD QUIT YOUR JOB

YOU'RE AT A FORK IN THE ROAD.

For a long time, I struggled to give people the advice to quit their job without anything lined up. I didn't want to ruin their lives. I didn't want to be that guy that pushed someone over the edge, only to find out later that they did a permanent nose-dive and that they'd have been better staying in their current situation, even if it wasn't ideal.

But then I had a revelation about why people read my work and why you're reading this book. You're probably reading this book because you're on the edge of quitting and you're looking for someone to push you over. You're on the high dive and everyone is waiting for you to jump. You know you need to jump, but for one reason or another, you're not making the leap.

Nobody ever emails me and says, "Hey Robbie, my life is going great. My career is sizzling hot. I just got a raise. Just saying hello."

People who reach out to me are usually at the all-time lowest points of their career and life. Their emails usually look like this: "Robbie, my life is in shambles. I hate my boss. I hate the office politics. I wish my boss would fire me. I would quit, but I'm scared. I'm also the sole income generator in my family, so I can't afford to miss a paycheck or I'll have to send my daughter to public school and my family will hate me forever if that happens. Can you help me?"

These days I'm all for pushing everyone over the edge. Trust me. I have no issues with it. Because I know the benefits of risk-taking.

I'm sure you have valid concerns, so think of it this way. You have two options:

Option 1: Continue through the pain and suffering of showing up to work every day, knowing that the work you're doing has no meaning.

Option 2: Live your life and career on your terms.

Let's be real. If you're reading this, you want to take option #2. Happiness is waking up every day and doing what you want to do. Happiness is going to sleep without worrying about work and bills. Happiness is being excited for the next day and not living for the weekend.

But for many us, the decision to quit seems financially irresponsible or downright impossible. You have a good source of income that you can't lose because you want to be "free and happy."

Reasons You Think You Can't Quit

If you're here thinking that real life gets in the way of success...you're right. Here are the top real-life situations that get in the way.

#1: Financial Responsibilities

When I see articles about "How to Travel the World on a Budget," I feel an urge to break something. I want to see someone write the article "How to Travel the World With a Full-Time Job, 1 Kid, Spouse, School Loans and a Mortgage You Can't Afford."

That article doesn't exist.

Most of those articles falsely assume that everyone's single, childless, and debt-free. Which leads to...you on the beach, broke. There isn't a worse feeling than sitting on a beach and not being able to afford the overpriced coconut drink from the beach vendor when you're dying of thirst.

Let's talk about the unexpected problems real life likes to lob your way.

You know what I'm talking about. Paying too much for a house you shouldn't have bought, marrying someone who doesn't like working or taking risks, and doing all this with a career path you don't like. Now *that's* my cup of tea.

Let's talk about everything that is preventing you from making a life breakthrough.

Let's talk about the SCREW YOU, I QUIT number. This is the amount of money you need in your bank account so you can look your boss in the eye and scream I QUIT!--without any doubts that your family will have a roof over their heads in a month.

Seriously, this is a great topic to discuss over Christmas eggnog.

"So, Jason... I was reading this random guy's article. He has this theory that everyone has a number of how much they need in their bank account before they can scream at their boss that they quit. Not to get too personal... but... I'm curious. What's your SCREW YOU, I QUIT number?"

Now *that's* an enjoyable Christmas.

Money buys you one thing: freedom to fail without your world collapsing. It doesn't buy you success. It doesn't buy you happiness. It buys you the freedom to screw it all up and have nothing catastrophic happen to you as a result.

#2: Parenting Responsibilities

"Thanks for paying the electricity bill, Mom." Said no kid ever.

I had a daughter recently. I was semi-complaining to a co-worker how hard it is to work and have a kid. He scoffed at me and said "HA! One kid? Man, you have it easy. Try three kids. You're playing on easy mode. Do you want to hear about my day yesterday with my kids?"

I never opened my mouth again about how hard life is with a kid. I will say this about children, though. Children are logistical nightmares.

Before Kid: Attend my favorite networking event at 6 p.m. once a month.

After Kid: No more attending networking events.

#3: Extended Friends And Family

"UGH. Jane just invited me to her Christmas party. I hate her boring-ass Christmas parties, plus it's all the way in the suburbs. I really don't want to go. Plus, I don't know what to get her for Christmas."

I heard this as I was walking outside a few days ago.

First off, screw Jane and her Christmas party that no one ever wants to go to but gets peer pressured into.

Second off, I find Christmas parties in the suburbs more enjoyable because there is usually more space.

Anyway, I digress. I live in the city while the rest of my family lives in the suburbs. So when my mom says to come over and eat some dinner with the rest of the family, naturally I'm excited to see them. However, that also means that my entire day to work on various projects disappears.

Do I love my mother? Of course. Do I love my brother, sister and their kids? Of course. Am I lucky that we get to sit down and enjoy each other's company? Of course. Does her inviting me over entirely screw the only time I have to work on some things that would advance my career? Of course it does.

#4: Fear Of The Unknown

I sent out a survey that 1,000 people in a career and life crossroads filled out. Their #1 fear of quitting their wretched jobs and getting better ones was that they *were afraid that they wouldn't like their next job.*

These people are the most unhappy bunch I've ever come across. And they're afraid that they might not get along with their new manager!

I still can't believe it. It's not like it was a multiple-choice survey, either. They could have written anything, yet 80% of them said the same thing.

CHAPTER THREE

QUESTION-AND-ANSWER TIME

I ALWAYS LIKE PRESENTATIONS WHEN THE Q&As ARE DONE in the middle or beginning of a presentation.

Now that we're most of the way through Chapter 1, let's have an impromptu Robbie-asks-Robbie Q&A session.

Question: Should I have my next job lined up before I quit?

The modest answer:

If you 100% can't afford a gap in pay or just can't risk being unemployed, then yes, get another job lined up before you quit.

Robbie's honest answer:

Here is where the world gets unfair and cruel.

Opportunities have a tendency to show up in the craziest places. A mentee of mine quit his job without anything lined up. It was the happiest day of his life since he was so miserable.

Two weeks later, an old friend of his said he was coming to the US, but he'd be three hours away from him and could only meet during the week.

My mentee said screw it and drove down to see him.

Six weeks later he moved to Colombia to work at his friend's company. All because he drove three hours during the week to catch up with his friend. If he had been employed, he would have never gone to see him.

That's why I say the world is cruel.

Sure. Wait until another job is lined up. But just know that random opportunities are way less likely to happen.

Question: Hi, Robbie. It must be easy for you to write a book about quitting when you don't have to worry about money. The rest of us have to worry about money, because we have expenses and children to take care of. I CAN'T take the risk of quitting. I just can't. I know I'm going to finish your book and be in the same spot I was before. I'm not risking the safety of my family for any reason. I don't have actually I have a question. I just wanted to tell you that.

I like to ask myself hard questions.

Nice to meet you and thanks for judging me when you don't know anything about me. I'll blame it on my editor for not filtering this "question" out, but hey, let me tackle this question head on.

You know how in the preface I talked about how your game of musical chairs is going to end eventually? You have no control of when the music ends; you just know it's going to stop. When it does end, you might find a chair or you might have the chair pulled from under you at the last second.

When the chair gets pulled from you at the last second, you can either fall flat on your ass and struggle to get back up, or you can have multiple options ready for you because you've been preparing for the game to end for a long time.

So my answer to your "question" is that your game of music chairs is going to end any day now. Could be tomorrow or 20 years from now.

The "I can't do anything because I need to support my family" attitude is going to kill you. In fact, it's an excuse. Don't wait for the music to stop on its own.

SECTION TWO -
SURVIVAL MODE

CHAPTER FOUR

BROKE TRIP TO ALDI

ONE DAY I WAS SHOPPING AT ALDI AS A COLLEGE STUDENT with only a few dollars to my name. I remember having to take a few things out of my box because I didn't have enough to buy everything I wanted. I was in between paychecks. I had less than $10 to my name.

I was broke.

I still remember exactly how I felt on the way back to my apartment. I was quiet and deep in my own thoughts. It was the first time I thought to myself, *I will never let this happen again.* I would never let myself get to the point where I had to make life decisions in line at a discount grocery store.

It was a sickening feeling I could feel deep in my stomach.

I told myself that I was going to be completely independent and I would do it all by myself. I had no choice.

I never wanted to feel that way ever again. I wasn't going to let myself down and I wasn't going to let my parents down. I needed to help them, not the other way around.

So what was the solution to make sure I was never this broke ever again?

The answer was clear: Work my ass off 24/7. I needed to work more, because working more = more money. More money = rent payments, food and tuition payments. I needed more money to be independent. I couldn't rely on anyone but myself.

I only thought one to two months ahead. I didn't think about where I'd be two to four years from then. I wasn't smart enough to do that. I was in survival mode, not "where do I see myself in five years" mode.

I started applying everywhere on campus at Purdue.

Within three months, I had three different jobs and was working 30-35 hours a week in addition to attending school full-time. I woke up at 8:00 a.m. and usually got home at 11:00 p.m. These were all standard office and student IT jobs. Answer phones, fix printers, do your homework when you have nothing else to do. My third job was working at a small ethnic grocery store.

My plan to support myself (if barely) worked. My next step was to find a great career in the IT industry.

When I graduated, I found myself in the same predicament as before. I was an average student with no connections in the corporate world. I knew no one who could open doors for me. I had to find a way to do it myself.

I didn't really have any strategies to landing an awesome career. Scratch that, I had one strategy:

Work my ass off.

Cast a wide net, and something has to hit. That was my strategy.

I went to every job fair, even if the job fair was just for women or for African Americans. I got weird looks, but I didn't care. The recruiters still talked to me. All I wanted was face time.

I sent follow-up emails and applied for every internship and job that I could.

It was the only way I knew how.

It worked. It had to work. There was no way it couldn't work.

I had joined a group at Purdue called Purdue Diversity Organization (PDO). By senior year, I was the director of the organization. We called high school seniors to let them know they had been accepted into Purdue University and would answer any questions they had. About 90% of the time, it was just the high school student screaming in excitement on the other end of the phone because we called them before they received their official acceptance letters.

There I met a wonderful woman named Antonia (Toni) Munguia, the Associate Director of Admissions responsible for this group. She was one of the very first people I met who actually cared about me and wanted me to succeed.

Senior year I had my head down applying and interviewing. I had two internships under my belt, including one with Dell, which was one of the hottest companies at the time.

A big job fair was coming up. Toni asked me if I wanted to help a recruiter at Accenture set up an informational session the day before the job fair. My response was: Accenture? Never heard of the company, but sure. I think they do consulting, and I'm not really sure what a consultant does. But I will definitely be there. I called off work and arrived the next day to help the recruiter.

This connection gave me the opportunity to meet the recruiter before the job fair. I still went to the job fair and asked to speak specifically to her. I said hello again and she made sure to get me an interview.

I was ecstatic. I became obsessed with a company I didn't know existed two days prior.

I pulled out all the big guns. I brought in five letters of recommendation specifically tailored for Accenture to my first interview. Yes, that's right. Five. Every job I ever worked at, plus the entire Purdue admissions office signed a recommendation letter. It's safe to say that I wasn't messing around.

I had no choice.

I had to make this happen.

I didn't just want this job. I needed this job.

It turned out Accenture was looking for technology graduates who didn't mind working until 7 p.m. every workday. I was a perfect fit. I got an offer.

I had 19 first-round interviews with other companies and ended with four job offers. (That's 15 rejections if you're counting.) Accenture was the clear winner. I started work two weeks after I graduated. I would have started the day after I graduated if they had let me.

I didn't need a break. I didn't even know how to take a break. It went against everything I stood for. My attention was solely trained on advancing my career in the best and fastest way possible.

This went on for about 8 years. For 8 years, I worked every single day I could. Nights, weekends, you name it. I was working whether it was for another company or when I quit my job to start my own company. I was working even when all my work was done. It didn't matter. I found work. I always had my head down. I was one of the most reliable and loyal people you could ever meet.

I didn't realize that the same strategy that had helped me get out of a rut at Purdue was now hurting me. I was too deep in it to understand what I was doing wrong.

Driving myself to the brink of burnout didn't stop me from doing good work in the short term, but I didn't have the bandwidth to think long-term. I was ignoring all my personal goals aside from making money.

It wasn't until recently I figured out that I've done enough surviving. Maybe now I should focus on living and start thinking five years ahead, instead of one to two months ahead.

But all of us will need to use short-term survival thinking to get through rough patches at one point or another. There is a time and place for it. Even now, every time I pass an Aldi, it always humbles me and also generates motivation to succeed even further.

Being broke at Aldi was the best thing to ever happen to me. It gave me a fire under my ass I didn't know existed.

Survival Mode

An interesting thing happens when you dive in headfirst after quitting. Your mentality changes. You stop worrying about what you're doing next weekend, and you start worrying about how you're going to get paid by next weekend.

You need to strap on your survival thinking. Though it's not wise to spend years in survival mode, it will serve you well in your time of need, drawing on your hidden stores of ingenuity and helping you break barriers. When in survival mode, the impossible becomes possible.

CHAPTER FIVE

INTRO TO SURVIVAL MODE

"Survival mode is a video game mode in which the player must continue playing for as long as possible without dying in an uninterrupted session while the game presents them with increasingly difficult waves of challenges." - Wikipedia

NO ONE TALKS ABOUT THE HARDSHIPS.

All you hear about is the success.

What you don't hear about is how people survived before they succeeded.

In this section, I'm going to teach you survival mode for the real world. Every day will get harder, and every challenge will be unannounced and almost impossible to solve by yourself.

In this chapter, I'm going to cover finances, time management, and mental management. These are key skills to master before you quit your job. Once you're competent in these areas, you can survive anything—including several months of unemployment.

You don't need to bet the farm to win. But you're going to have to sacrifice a few goats. Survival mode is about understanding what goats aren't going to survive and which ones are.

Let's do this.

CHAPTER SIX

FINANCIALS 101

I HAD 500 DOLLARS IN MY BANK ACCOUNT.

It was hovering at that amount for a long time no matter what I did. I bought fewer things and saved more money. I stopped going out on weekends. Somehow, someway, I always ended up with just $500 in my account.

One day I attended a large conference. The keynote speaker said:

"Be bold. You have to take risks to advance. Be your own brand. You have to stand out."

I'm sitting there, looking at this guy and thinking to myself, "Easy for you to say, buddy. You want me to be bold and risky with $500 in my bank account? I'd rather be safe with $500 in the bank than be bold with no money in my account."

Being bold wasn't an option for me. He was inspirational, but I still felt helpless.

The next person went up onto the stage and talked about how courageous the previous presenter had been for taking a huge leap and quitting their job. "Give me a break," I thought to myself. "That guy had money in the bank. If I had been in their shoes I'd have quit three years ago."

I was bitter and jealous. It seemed like everyone was flying by me and I had a four-ton anchor tied to my feet. I couldn't take any risks. I had plenty of potential, but I was tied down by my financials.

Here's what I did.

I tracked my finances like a madman every single day. After three rejections from the bank, I figured out a way to refinance my mortgage. I cancelled services that I didn't need. I disposed of a rental property that was losing money every month. I changed my payment plan for student loans so it aligned with my new financial goals. I became as financially lean as I could be.

The only reason I hadn't taken these steps before was that I didn't think I could. I honestly thought I had no choices, when in reality I had plenty of them. They just weren't clear to me.

Now I'll teach you how to calculate what you can do.

Disclaimer: Everyone's situation is unique and risk tolerance also varies wildly. The purpose of this section is to give you a guideline to base your decisions on.

Survival Mode: Money Management 101

How you manage money in normal, salary-earning mode is very different than how you should manage money in survival mode. In the first, a consistent income automatically arrives in your bank account every two weeks. In the second, you probably don't know where your next paycheck is coming from.

So you need to change your mentality.

Two things I want you to learn in this chapter:

1. How to budget your money
2. How to make more money

Let's talk about budgeting money. Budgeting money isn't always about saving money. It's about setting expectations for what you need to survive without dramatically changing your lifestyle.

What this means is that you don't have to move your family to a trailer park to make this happen. But it does mean that you should know exactly how much money you're going to spend on your mortgage in the next six months—and if there are ways to reduce that cost while you go through this process.

Rule #1: Fear fixed expenses. They will be the first thing to cut your entrepreneurial career short.

Have you ever gone to a grocery story and felt proud of yourself because you got the generic laundry detergent instead of the brand-name detergent?

Then the mortgage payment comes. Followed by the car bills, student loans, electricity, cell phone bills and whatever other fixed expenses you've managed to take on.

Now you don't feel so good about yourself.

The $2 you saved on detergent is nothing compared to the thousands of dollars that come out of your bank account.

Fixed expenses are the hardest to change. I can decide to eat in instead of eating out, but I can't decide to not pay my mortgage payment or only decide to pay half. It doesn't work like that.

Rule #2: Every dollar must be accounted for and budgeted for in the next six months.

I don't want you to read this lightly. You must know where you spend every dollar every day and how much you need to survive the next six months while maintaining your lifestyle.

I'm not just talking about looking at a report at the end of the month and seeing what *categories* you spent your money on. I'm talking about reviewing every single transaction manually, and, most importantly, understanding what your fixed expenses add up to every month.

Understand your fixed expenses to the dollar.

- Do not auto-import your bank account into any kind of financial software. There are plenty of tools that sync with your bank to give you up-to-date information and reporting. They are great, but not for people who are in survival mode. You should evaluate every transaction you made in the month/week prior.
- Something crazy happens when you see the individual transactions appear over and over (as opposed to seeing just one summary statement.) It helps you physically feel the departure of each dollar.

Rule #3: Only budget money you have, not money "you're supposed to" get.

If you don't have the money with you or in your bank account, assume you'll never get it. Your friend who owes you money? Assume he'll never pay you back. The grandma you're expecting to keel over any day now, and you're 97% sure she put you in the will, will probably live to be the oldest woman in the world. If you don't have it, don't budget it. It's that simple.

Rule #4: Assume you're going to make $0 in the next six months.

Your direct deposit at your salary job was consistent and dependable to come in every two weeks.

It's OK to plan on making money in the future. Welcome to the new world in which nobody owes you anything. Money is inconsistent and undependable. Even when contracts are signed and money is owed, the money is not guaranteed.

If you already have something lined up before you quit, good for you.

Rule #5: Expect your job search to take at least six months, from the moment you decide that you're getting a new job.

On the safe side, budget a year. Even if you have a marketable skill set, it can take this long. Everything takes longer when you need it the most—just remember that. Even with a smooth interviewing process, it can easily take three months. Don't underestimate.

Rule #6: Budget at least a year of savings in cash for an emergency fund.

Expect the unexpected. Just because you're in survival mode doesn't mean that you can't plan for catastrophes. Put yourself in a good place.

- Single? You can budget six months.
- Married and no children? One year.

- Married with children? 18 months.

I always have a laugh with my wife when we talk about where our money goes, sometimes very mysteriously. We don't do drugs. We don't party. We don't gamble. By every measure, we are reasonable with our money. But when we add up the amount we spent the month prior, it's always higher than we expect it to be.

Fixed expenses + unplanned expenses add up *really* quickly. It's important you adjust how much money you think you're going to spend to reflect the amount you actually spend.

These books forever changed my financial literacy:

- *I Will Teach You To Be Rich* by Ramit Sethi
- *MONEY Master the Game*: 7 Simple Steps to Financial Freedom by Tony Robbins
- I read reddit.com/r/personalfinance every single day -- this is a truly amazing community of people. Read all the posts and learn how these people think.
- I bought the You Need a Budget software (http://youneedabudget.com), which is the only finance tool I've ever really stuck with. A true game-changer in how you think about money. If nothing else, read about the methodology. It's something I wish I used 10 years ago. My wife and I sit down twice a month to go over it. It's opened up the world for both of us.

The first thing that needs to change is your expectation of what's to come. Expectations of income, relationships and business models. You will be challenged in all three.

Rule #7: Reduce the number of people who can ruin your life with one major decision.

"I don't like it when one person can make or break me. A boss. A publisher. A TV producer. A buyer of my company. At any one point I've had to kiss ass to all of the above. I hate it. I will never do it again."--James Altucher

Ahh, yes. Wise words from my favorite person, James Altucher. First, write down all the people that can ruin your life with one decision. For everyone you list, write down a way you can reduce the risk of them ruining your life. Disclaimer: This doesn't mean that you *have* to work for yourself to be happy. I always like to say that dream jobs aren't real. It's about the dream situation.

The dream situation is, you guessed it: To live your life and career on your own terms. And yes, this means making enough money to support your dream situation. The situation might entail freedom *from* work. Perhaps working remotely instead of being in the office every day. This might mean working hard Monday to Thursday and having Friday off. This might mean being able to work with people you learn from and appreciate you. This might mean being able to travel every week. Everyone's dream situation is different.

But even if you're not angling to start your own business, there's a 99.9% chance you still need to quit your job. If your name isn't Anthony Bourdain, AKA the man who gets paid to travel and eat food all over the world, then I don't believe that you're getting paid to do what you love right now.

The dream situation is something you probably think about all the time. Don't ignore it.

CHAPTER SEVEN

TIME MANAGEMENT 101

WHETHER YOU'RE PRODUCTIVE OR NOT, YOU WILL STILL BE getting paid at your 9-5. You have no incentive to become more productive at work. Because the more productive you are, the more work you will have to do. So, even though you attempt to become more productive, even if you don't increase your productivity, nothing major will happen.

This all changes when you stop getting paid every two weeks from your salaried job. Productivity and time management become *real* issues. You need to become more productive to make more money or build a bigger business. Now, productivity and time management are *real*.

This is also relevant if you're not quitting, but you're doing a side hustle. You should be looking to make more time to spend on your side gig.

Here is how you do it:

Step 1: Mentally Separate Yourself From Your Current Job

This requires a mind shift. A big mind shift.

You need to act like an independent consultant. An independent consultant is a person who is self-employed and gets paid by working at other companies on a contract. An independent consultant is unique in the sense that they can work on one client or multiple clients simultaneously, but it's their responsibility to find clients to work on. If they don't have a client, they don't get paid. It's that simple.

Achieving this goal is a big task and requires a different frame of mind.

Here is what you need to tell yourself:

You are no longer Michael Smith the full-time employee of Acme Corporation. You are now Michael Smith, the independent consultant who was contracted to perform a specific set of activities. Acme Corporation is no longer your full-time employer; it is your client who pays you for every hour that you work.

You have a six-month contract with Acme Corporation in which they pay you for 40 hours of your time each week. Any time worked outside of these 40 hours must be pre-approved by the client.

Here's the difference between the full-time employee and the independent consultant.

Michael Smith, full-time employee:

- Hired to perform one activity, often gets involved in many other activities not specifically related to job function.
- Jack of all trades, master of none.

- Expected to work all day and night, including weekends even if the work doesn't require it.
- Pay is based on salary, not the value of his services.
- Attends all required employee meetings, whether they directly pertain to his work or not.
- Has a secure job for a successful company and doesn't need to look for next gig.
- Doesn't take responsibility for something that went wrong if it wasn't his fault.

Michael Smith, independent consultant:

- Hired to perform one activity. Contractually not allowed to work on other work specifically not defined in his contract.
- Master of a specific function; knows a little bit of everything else, but is known for his specific function skill.
- Expected to complete the deliverable based on agreed hours in the contract – and if he goes over those hours, it will require more difficult conversations and approvals in the budget to perform those activities.
- Hourly rate is determined on how valuable his specific skill is and how important his skill is to the organization.
- Attends few to no company meetings so he can focus on what he was contracted to do.
- Forced to continually look for new gigs and maintain his relationships with other companies to see what opportunities they have coming up.
- Will stop getting paid once this contract ends, so is always thinking two steps ahead and planning for next gig.

- Takes responsibility for something that went wrong, even if it was the client's fault. Puts an action plan together to fix the issue and fixes the issue once the plan is approved.

See the difference between the two? They were both hired to do one thing. However, one person ends up getting pulled in a million directions while the independent consultant has a clear vision of what his job is.

The full-time employee Michael Smith has more stability than the independent consultant. But since he doesn't have to look for new jobs, he isn't expanding his network and forming new relationships.

How To Work No More Than 40 Hours Per Week

Everything you have ever been taught pairs success and effort. To succeed, you need to give 110% effort. Get to work early, leave late; do the jobs that no one else wants to do; be the leader when everyone else is following. Lead by example.

I want you to stop doing all of that.

- Stop showing up to work earlier than everyone else. Show up on time and leave on time.
- Don't do the jobs no one else wants to do. Do the job you were hired to do.
- Don't lead when everyone else is following. Let someone else lead this time.
- Stop saying yes to every work assignment that comes to you. Learn to say no. Better yet, learn to avoid situations where people ask you to do more work.
- Stop offering new suggestions to improve a process. Nothing will change at your company besides YOU.

- Stop coming through the front door. Come through the back door and be as invisible as possible.
- While you're at it, take that stupid inspirational quote off your cubicle, too. Newsflash, you're not Winston Churchill. You're a miserable worker who currently has no idea what to do with your life. For God's sake, look at what you are reading right now.

Today is the day you actively pursue mediocrity in your current job and you're going to love every second of it.

My horror stories of being underappreciated at work are actually great news for you. I've thoroughly tested the waters and found that you can do (what you would consider) a mediocre job and your employer will be satisfied with your work.

You need a B on your report card. That's it. Not a B+, and not a B-. You just need to shoot for the 3.0.

Right now you're shaking your head and saying, "But Robbie, I'm not the type of person that goes for Bs. I either go hard or go home!"

As take a lot of dedication, energy, and hard work. A typical student who gets As in every single class often has no time for anything else. If your goal is to keep advancing in your current company and to achieve greatness at that company, then you probably should be reading something else.

Step 2: Be Unbelievably, Unrealistically, Foolishly Awesome At Saying No

I've read every article on how to say NO. Everyone says to say NO more often. I know the more I say yes, the more I lose focus. I've told everyone I know to say NO more often.

I used to be the master of saying NO.

Until someone convinced me to say yes to help them build a billion-dollar company. I said no 10 times. He persisted. The 11th time I said yes.

The company imploded three months later.

That "yes" cost me three months of my time that I can't get back.

I was actually glad it imploded so I could re-focus on myself.

I'm sick of living someone else's dream.

The only lesson learned from this mistake? Get better at saying NO. Kind of like innocent until proven guilty. I'm just going to default to NO.

Here's your new script for saying NO.

Let's go over some situations.

Boss: "Melissa - We're doing an all-night Hackathon next Monday. Do you want to plan and run it?"

You: "Oh, man. I would love to. But, I have plans with my family that night. Also, I really want to focus on my core activities. I have a lot going on. I don't think I would be able to make it any good. I think Mark would be great for it though. Let me see if he wants to do it. Sounds exciting!"

Replace "all-night hackathon" with any activity that isn't directly related to your job. The answer is always "Oh, man, I would love to, but I can't." Always.

The framework for saying NO is simple. If someone is asking you to do something that isn't 100% related to the core activities of your salary-paying job, then the answer is NO.

Think of your annual performance review and how that activity will be viewed. No one will give you a raise because you planned the hackathon. It even sounds silly if you use that as a talking point.

Coworker: "Our division lost money, but hey, I spent three weeks planning that hackathon!"

Sounds stupid. Because it is.

Say YES if an opportunity:

- Helps you build new connections
- Helps you build a new marketable skillset
- Helps you make more money
- Helps you open doors to potential new opportunities
- Helps you build a stronger relationship with someone who might be able to help you in the future

Everything else is a NO.

> "Beware of the person who gives advice, telling you that a certain action on your part is 'good for you' while it is also good for him, while the harm to you doesn't directly affect him." – Nassim Taleb

Use the same rubric when it comes to "working for free."

There are some people who tell you that you should never work for free no matter what. This is what happens when you look at the world in a one-dimensional way.

You have to ask yourself, "What are the opportunities that can happen because of this?"

If working for free meets any point on the rubric above, then go for it. Obviously use your best judgment so you don't get taken advantage of, but for the most part, if the opportunity is great, take it.

Step 3: Free Up Time At Work By Improving Your Communication Style

Here is what I do:

Be amazingly quick on responses. I adopted the five sentences or less policy. If I can answer a question in less than two minutes and type less than five sentences, I answer it right away.

Resist the urge to reply back to emails that don't need your input. If the email doesn't start off with addressing you specifically, then there is an 80%-90% chance you don't need to reply back to it. Replying takes energy, and most of the time the person who the email is addressed to is the person responsible for answering. If that person wants to ask you a question, then they will ask you. Until then, keep your mouth shut and move on to the next email.

Estimate how long a task should take and multiply that number by three. This is a trick used by software devel opers because in theory a task should only take a specific amount of time. But these estimates are normally done as if you live in a bubble and don't have outside influences that delay when a task can get completed. The system is down, Pam keeps bothering you, an unexpected urgent task lands on your desk, etc. So if someone sends you a task that should take you one hour that you can start on Tuesday morning, the number you communicate is that it will take you three hours and you will get it done in three days—on Thursday.

Send your boss these two emails per week. You'll both improve your relationship and produce the best work you've ever done:

Email #1: What you plan on getting done this week

Email #2: What you actually got done this week

Limit yourself to schedule forty hours of planned work.

Here's what email #1 looks like:

> *Subject: My plan for the week*
>
> *Jane, after reviewing my activities, here is my plan for the week in order of priority. Let me know if you think I should re-prioritize:*
>
> *Planned major activities for the week*
>
> *Complete project charter for Project X*
>
> *Finish the financial analysis report that was started last week*
>
> *Kick off Project X – requires planning and prep documentation creation (scheduled for Thursday)*
>
> *Open items that I will look into, but won't get finished this week*
>
> *Coordinate activities for year-end financial close*
>
> *Research Product Y for our shared service team*
>
> *Let me know if you have any comments. Thank you!*
>
> *-- Robbie*

Right now you're thinking: "But Robbie, my boss is the one that assigns me the work! He obviously knows what I'm working on! Why would I send him this email?"

You are so wrong that it makes me want to throw up. Let me clue you in on a secret: your boss barely remembers what he did this week, let alone what you've been up to this entire time. How self-centered of you to think he knows everything you're spending your time on at work.

"But Robbie, I have at least sixty hours of work to do. How in the world am I going to do it in forty hours? It's impossible; our group is so busy right now."

Take a look at my sample email #1. Did you break down your tasks into must-have vs. nice-to-have? Or did you put everything into the must-be-done category?

Did you schedule yourself for sixty hours a week or did your boss schedule you for sixty hours of week? I want you to think about this.

Email #2 on Friday: What you got done this week.

It looks something like this:

Completed this week

- *Completed Report X*
- *Started the planning for the big project*
- *Finished the month-end analysis and sent to financial controller for review*
- *Created a first draft of the project charter, which is currently being reviewed by PM team*

Open items

- *I have some questions about the start date of Project Y, but should get confirmation by Tuesday morning*
- *We need Report X signed off by end of day next Wednesday. Can you follow up with Jane to get this signed off?*

That is all for now. Have a great weekend.

-- Robbie

This report does two things very well: it provides closure to the week and gives your manager an idea of what you can complete in a week. In other words, it sets expectations!

Tips for Email #2:

- Focus on what you completed first and open issues second.
- Always end Friday on a good note. If you have issues, bring them up on Monday morning. Don't stress your boss out all weekend, because it will stress you out as well.

This Friday report is so simple and effective; it's amazing that people just leave on Friday without sending this report. It changes everything.

Now you're wondering, "Well, what would I do with all this new energy and time?"

In the following chapters I will tell you exactly where you can spend this new-found freedom. It will be spent on activities that you want to do and how to actively get where you want to be. Right now, you just need to know it won't be spent on your current job.

CHAPTER EIGHT

WHEN IN SURVIVAL MODE, YOU'LL NEED TO MAKE SOME mental shifts. First of all, let's attack the guilt you're likely feeling about abandoning your company in pursuit of your dream.

But what about loyalty?

I was the most loyal of them all. I was the golden retriever of corporate loyalty. I was sipping so much Kool-Aid I could have sworn the Kool-Aid guy was following me around just to make sure I had enough Kool-Aid to drink. I worked twice as hard as everyone else.

On one particular occasion, it was time to discuss our perfor-mance evaluations and raises. I thought for sure my work ethic and my loyalty would get me the highest performance rating and the biggest raise. After all, the people I took care of were going to take care of me in return. I had it all figured out.

Then I got a "meets expectation" rating and a measly 2.1% raise. The company's reasoning behind this? "The economy was bad," and I "needed to work on my functional industry skills." That was it.

All of those pages of self-evaluation I filled out for my portion of the performance review really didn't matter. That entire year I had hustled and gone above and beyond the call of duty. Let's not forget about how loyal I was!

For a long time, I did whatever a manager asked of me regardless of whether it was in my job description or not.

I finally figured out that I was actually hurting my career by being so helpful. How about the time I worked until 3:00 a.m. for weeks straight to finish a project no sane person would have completed at all, given so few resources?

Or what about that time I took an international flight to help with a project on one day's notice? That must have translated into a huge raise, or at least a gift card, right?

All I heard was silence, and all I felt was exhausted from taking on the impossible. What's worse is that I kept trying the same thing, over and over, hoping it would yield a different result. That's called insanity.

For the record, I would have taken a $20 gift card to Olive Garden if it meant my managers acknowledging my worth. Hell, do you know how many unlimited breadsticks I can get with $20? Nothing says, "We appreciate your hard work" like a gift card to Olive Garden.

My point is that loyalty doesn't matter. It doesn't matter one bit. What matters the most is that you get the right work done for the right people. I also found that it actually doesn't matter how long you work. No one will give you a better raise if you work late for two weeks straight.

Loyalty should be earned, not implied.

I've learned to be loyal to the people I work with and not the company I work for. There are a handful of people who have earned my loyalty:

- The director who immediately honored my last-minute request to not join a project for personal reasons.
- The career counselor who found me a position in the company, which allowed me to stop traveling and work from home. She did this despite the fact it directly resulted in my losing her as a counselor, and that it meant she had to replace my spot on her project.
- The executive who lobbied to get me an office when everyone else wanted me to sit in a cubicle (a small example, but representative of the types of things he did over a long period).

I found three people who have proven that they are willing to go out of their way to help me, even if the result of their assistance is detrimental to their own goals.

This doesn't mean I hate or distrust everyone else I worked with. My mentality is that I trust everyone I meet until they prove to me they shouldn't be trusted. I have gotten burned many times by adopting this way of thinking, but I still think it's the right approach.

Learn How To Be Less Miserable—Maybe Even Happy—In The Months Before You Quit

I always thought I had a clear mind. That is, until I actually had a clear mind and knew what that meant.

I was able to clear my mind by doing two things:

- **Forgiving others who screwed me**
- **Forgiving myself**

Forgiving people is probably the hardest thing I've ever done. Especially when they don't deserve to be forgiven. I'm asking you to forgive others who wronged you. Whether it was personally or professionally.

Stop hating them. Stop being jealous of them. Let it go. Come to terms with it. Don't try to understand why they did this to you. They did it for their own reasons.

Secondly, forgive yourself. In the beginning of my career as a consultant, I was so hard on myself. The absolute worst time for me was year-end reviews with my managers. They were always positive reviews, except I always received one or two constructive criticisms. I always left those meetings hating myself, even if I got the highest rating.

I didn't need to be perfect, but I was just so concerned with how others perceived me. I don't know why, it was just the way it was.

So what I'm asking you is to give yourself a break. Forgive yourself for making that mistake at your job that made everyone including executive leadership mad at you.

You know that queasy feeling you get in your stomach when you see another person who you personally or professionally let down and are unable to look in the eye anymore? It's okay. We all have that feeling once in a while. Some let it stay with them. Some forgive themselves and let it go.

Forgive yourself for not taking that job when you had the chance. You thought you did the right thing at the time. It's OK. Let it go. There's nothing you can do about it now. So move on.

The problem with miserable people is that they operate with severe tunnel vision. They aren't able to look at their job holistically. So instead of understanding issues and seeking solutions, they plod forward with their heads down, learning nothing.

Here's how you become a great observer.

At your next meeting I want you to go out of your way to not talk. Pretend you're just a fly on the wall. Even if you know the answer to the question, just shut up. Even if you want to add something to what someone else said, don't.

Just sit there and listen.

Look around to see who's on their phone. Look to see who's multitasking and answering their email. Look to see which of your colleagues are texting each other across the room, exchanging super secret information.

Observe how long people talk during meetings. Could that person who just spent five minutes explaining a problem have explained it in thirty seconds? What about that other person who just HAS to add their commentary? Were their comments relevant and necessary?

Observe the times you receive emails from your colleagues. Who consistently sends email after 5:00 p.m. or on weekends? Who works from home the most? Who comes in to work the most?

Observe others' behaviors. Let it all sink in.

How does this help you become happier?

It helps you understand your current work situation better. Your goal is to understand what your real role is at work and to understand how others work.

There is a good chance that if you're still reading this with interest, you have tunnel vision. You have an inability to understand where you fit in at work. Do you really understand what your role is?

It's not that serious.

> *"You develop an instant global consciousness, a people orientation, an intense dissatisfaction with the state of the world, and a compulsion to do something about it. From out there on the moon, international politics look so petty. You want to grab a politician by the scruff of the neck and drag him a quarter of a million miles out and say, 'Look at that, you son of a bitch.'"*
>
> *—Edgar Mitchell*

I actually hate quotes. I hate quoting quotes. I just couldn't find a way to say it better than Edgar did.

When you're "in it," it's easy to believe that your job is so important that you have to put all of your energy into it. If you're like me, you take in your pride in your work.

When you commit to doing something, you do whatever it takes to get it done so you don't let your colleagues down. This is how the tunnel vision begins.

I'm going to let you in on a little secret...

Are you ready?

This might blow your mind, but...

It's not that serious.

Yes, I'm talking to you. What you're working on right now is not that important in the whole scheme of things. I know it seems super important, but it really isn't. I know you can't possibly let your colleagues down. I know you need the money. I know this job is your lifeline right now.

Take a minute to read Edgar's quote again. I want you to take a look at what you're working on from the perspective of the moon.

How important is what you're doing at work now? Is it worth working overtime? Is it worth the constant stress you put on yourself? Is your job providing actual value to the world? The last time you got into an argument with someone at work, was it real anger or petty anger? Could you justify your hatred all the way from the moon?

Is it that serious?

CHAPTER NINE

OFFLINE PROFESSIONAL NETWORKING
101

WHAT ARE THE BENEFITS OF PROFESSIONAL Networking?

I tried to rephrase this question without sounding like your college counselor, but I couldn't do it no matter how hard I tried. Getting involved and putting yourself out there is truly the only way to create opportunities for yourself.

If you want to quit your job, you need to learn how to network before you even think the next snarky thought about your boss. In this chapter, you'll learn how to open doors to better places.

You'll learn how to build a better career, to make more money, and to create long-lasting friendships.

Warning: Networking is a long-term affair. If you're in it for the quick sale, you're going to be sadly disappointed. It just doesn't work that way.

There is someone out there who needs your skills as much as you need their resources, mentorship, or the experience you can gain from working with them. The trick is for you to be able to find one another.

How long does it take to build a network? That's a loaded question, so I'm going to simplify it for you. A real professional relationship happens when you see the same person on three different occasions within a three- to six-month period.

But first, a story.

How I Met James Altucher: How to Have Coffee with the Busiest Person in the World

"You're so annoying, Robbie." -- James Altucher

I idolized James Altucher. It is safe to say that I had a man crush. If you don't know James, he wrote one of the most popular posts on LinkedIn in 2014 about how you should quit your job.

Mine wasn't your normal man crush. He didn't have a body I wanted, nor did he necessarily have the job I wanted.

Have you ever seen someone on television or read someone's writing, and your first reaction was, "I MUST meet this person?" James taught me to bleed on the page. He single-handedly changed my writing style. Before James, I had always been afraid to write. One of the best stories I ever wrote in college, I actually plagiarized. That was the only way I could write anything good. Don't worry; I got caught.

James always said that if I ever wanted to become a decent writer, I had to write 500 words every day. In 2012, my New Year's resolution was to write a blog post every day. I wrote 200 posts that year. I forced myself to write. They mostly sucked. Most of the comments on my blog posts were corrections to my grammar.

That was the year I wrote the article, "Fire Me I Beg You," which eventually turned into a book. I wrote the article in 20 minutes. I told myself I couldn't leave the office until I wrote something.

I wrote about anything that was on my mind. I wrote about career advancement, sports, startups, mobile apps, food... I even wrote satire. I honestly can't tell you what my goal in writing these posts was. I didn't have a master plan. I just had something inside me that said, "Get it all out, man."

I knew one thing for certain, though. I knew that I had to meet James Altucher.

I tried everything. I offered to work for him for free. He responded to my first email, and then never responded again. I constantly wrote articles about him on my blog, just so he would notice the impact he was having on my writing. No luck.

I added him on Facebook. I followed him on LinkedIn. I joined his newsletter. I constantly tweeted and re-tweeted his posts. He would reply, but what I really wanted was for him to follow me. He never did.

I tried setting up a Mastermind dinner. I lured the most successful people I could find to that one dinner. I offered to pay for James's flight and hotel. Didn't work.

I tried different variations of these schemes for four years. Finally, I was going to New York for vacation and I'd heard he lived in New York.

Email Chain #1:

Robbie: I'm going to be in New York on Saturday. Let's have coffee.

James: I live far from New York.

Robbie: It's on my way to Boston. (It was completely out of my way.)

James: <No Response>

Email Chain #2:

Robbie: I'm going to New York. You're on the way. Can I buy you coffee?

James: I'm only available Friday, sorry.

Robbie: That's fine. I can make Friday work. How about 2:00 p.m.?

James: <No Response>

Email Chain #3:

Robbie: I'm going to come by at 2:00 p.m. on Friday. Does that work? Can you give me an address?

James: <No Response>

Robbie: (I sent him this tweet since I knew he was active on Twitter.)

@jaltucher still on for tomorrow? :) if not, no worries, can do it when more convenient!

James: @RobbieAb hey Robbie, I'm good. Want to make it noon instead? I have a podcast starting at 11 that should be done by noon.

Email Chain #4:

James: Here is the address to the coffee shop. See you at noon.

Robbie: See you there!

(Internally: "OMG. This is happening.")

I rented a car in Manhattan and got to the coffee shop three hours early. I couldn't risk being late. I was a nervous wreck. I wanted to do more research on James but I couldn't because my phone was running out of battery. I had no idea how to get back and needed the GPS. Instead I paid 50 cents for a local newspaper so I could calm down and kill time. I learned that no one is ever happy with how their city or town is being run.

He showed up. We never had coffee. He instead invited me to his house to do a podcast about how I take 250 coffee meetings a year. He tried to pay for my breakfast but I had already paid. I was the first person to ever be invited to his house. I met his wonderful wife Claudia.

We did the podcast. I gave him a gift.

He ended up writing an article about how persistent I was.

The funny thing is that before I drove to meet him, my wife told me that I should ask him to be on his podcast. I laughed and said to her, "I wish, but I don't want to waste his time." I didn't have to ask. He asked me.

I picked up my wife from the loading station at the Statue of Liberty. She asked to see the picture I took of all of us.

I never took a picture. I completely forgot. It didn't matter. I had met James Altucher. He was exactly what I expected and more. I didn't get to ask him any questions. He did all the talking.

Do yourself a favor. Find someone to admire. Invite them for a cup of coffee. If they don't respond at first, that's okay.

It only took me four years.

———

Your new #1 goal is to be—at most—two degrees of separation from the influencers in your industry. So identify them. Find the people that could potentially hire you. This is where you start.

This means you should either know the influencer firsthand or know someone who can connect you to that person.

Let me guess...that paragraph made you nervous.

Consider Yourself An Equal

I have a friend who hates bothering busy people. I once connected him with an influential contact. Let's call this influential person Michael. I did everything by the book. I asked Michael if he was willing to meet with my friend who needed deeper connections to find a better job. He said yes. Great.

I sent an email introducing both of them. A couple months later, I asked my friend how the meeting went.

Here's how the conversation went:

> **Me:** How did the conversation go with Michael?
>
> **Friend:** I sent him an email after you connected us. He never responded back.
>
> **Me:** Oh, I'm sorry. Did you follow up?
>
> **Friend:** Nah, I didn't want to annoy the guy. I know he's really busy. I don't want to be a bother.
>
> **Me:** I already talked with him. He said he'd meet with you. This wasn't a cold email. You just need to at least follow up one more time. This person keeps his word when he says yes. I created a warm environment for you, so you just need to be persistent with him to get the meeting.

Friend: Are you sure? Man, I really don't want to bother the guy. He's got so many things going on and I'm just going to annoy him.

Me: <Shaking my head> Well, you know what this person thinks now, right? Michael's thinking it wasn't important that you needed to meet with him, so he just ignored the original email. If it were important, you would have followed up at least once. You're right. He is too busy. He's too busy to meet with people who never really wanted to meet with him in the first place. Your loss.

Stop thinking about what this other person will think of you. Chances are if you don't follow up to a warm email, that person will think you never wanted to meet with them in the first place.

Which brings me to my main point:

If you think you are an equal, you will become an equal.

You are an equal to Michael. Even if Michael won four Nobel Peace Prizes, has 10 PhDs and shot a hole in one as a lefty. Even if you desperately need a job from Michael and Michael can make it happen.

Even if Michael is smarter, better looking, lives in a better neighborhood and buys islands because he's got nothing else to do with all his money. You are equal to him.

My point is: You have to believe you are an equal, or your relationships with influential people will fail. No one wants to do business with someone below them. You're not trying to do business with someone who has less credibility than you do, right?

How To Get Influential People To Help You

With a little hesitation that I might discredit this entire book by overpromising results, I'm going to quote the artist Pitbull.

"Ask for money, and get advice.

Ask for advice, get money twice."

This works like a charm for more reasons than one.

I was looking for a new gig and I identified a company I wanted to work for. I knew a senior-level director at this firm, and I was unsure if this person would refer me to the company or not based on our previous working relationship.

So I sent him an email asking about the pros and cons of working for this type of consulting company. I let him know I was looking for jobs at companies with the same structure.

He responded and let me know briefly about what it was like. He then told me of a job opening and said he would gladly refer me if I was interested.

Fantastic. What this did was allow me to save face if he didn't want to refer me. He could have just told me about what it was like working there.

So, let's just say you need to go in for the kill and ask someone for direct help.

All you need to remember is that people do business with people they know, like and trust. So next time you want to ask someone for help, ask yourself these three questions:

- Do they know me?
- Do they like me?
- Do they trust me?

If you answer yes to all three, go ahead and ask for help. If you can't answer yes to all three, you can still ask for help. But chances are they have no incentive to help you and your selfish requests for help.

What if they say no? Forgive them for not responding positively and forgive yourself for thinking you look stupid now. Learn from the experience. Let it go. Clear your mind. Rinse and repeat.

How To Get Influential People To Like You

Targeted outreach to someone you already admire is one tool in your networking toolkit. Now let's move on to more general networking strategies. I put together four steps:

> **Step 1:** Find your second home, fast. AKA: Build your community.

> **Step 2:** Utilize your existing network to strategically expand.

> **Step 3:** Acquire the tools and processes to maintain and grow your network.

> **Step 4:** Follow these general networking tips.

Step 1: Find Your Second Home, Fast. AKA: Build Your Community

Step 1.1: Put a plan together to build your community.

This activity requires a LinkedIn account. By now, you should know how important LinkedIn is for all things career-related. At this point, if you don't have a LinkedIn profile, you should stop reading and go back to posting quotes on your Instagram.

If you pay for a premium account, fantastic. If not, you can still accomplish all this without one.

Step 1.2: Write down the people you consider the top performers or the most professionally connected in your desired industry and city.

I use LinkedIn heavily to do my research.

Step 1.3: Email them.

The next best step is to email them with one simple question. So, you're probably thinking, "Well, that escalated quickly, Robbie. I haven't even met the person, and you want me to cold email them?"

The answer is yes.

Let's say you want to email Janet Davis, VP of a successful digital agency. Your email should contain two sentences.

> *Subject: Hi Janet – A good digital marketing event or organization that you could recommend?*
>
> *Body of Email:*
>
> *I'm looking for a high-quality networking group to be part of in the digital marketing space. Are there any you would recommend in the Chicago downtown or suburban area?*
>
> *Based on my research, you would be the best person to answer this question. Thank you!*
>
> *– Robbie*

This email is ideal for several reasons:

- It's under five sentences (so it's short and sweet).

- You have successfully presented yourself as someone who is genuinely curious to join a high-quality group.
- If she runs a networking group or event, she will recommend that you attend hers. Voila! This is your "in" to meeting Janet in a comfortable environment.
- You've shown that you have done research about her, which will make her more likely to respond.

Once you start your search, you should send at least five of these emails. You should also follow up if you don't hear back immediately.

Step 1.4: Plan B: Scope out the scene yourself.

If you don't get responses and don't know where else to get good recommendations about local events, this is your next option.

Find three types of events:

1. General meet & greet networking (network after work, speed networking)
2. General networking with an emphasis (The Chicago Black Professionals, Cheers for Moms, Chicago Technology LGBT, etc.)
3. Event/speaker-focused networking (think tech event with a speaker)

What event should you go to first?

I know this answer sounds simple, but trust me, it eludes many people.

1. Go to the event that has the people that you want to meet.

2. Go to the event that you have something in common with.

For example, if you are a graduate of Notre Dame University, and you had the option of going to the Digital Marketers in Chicago Meetup or the Notre Dame Digital Marketers in Chicago Meetup, which one are you going to attend?

The Notre Dame event. Your college alumni are the most likely to help you and connect you. The normal digital marketing group will be less likely to help you (at least initially) because they don't have any common bond with you.

Whatever you do, don't go to the event where you feel the most comfortable. Go to the event that will give you the most value.

Step 1.5: Attend.

Networking events get a bad rap. I hear the same thing over and over from people who don't like them: "Oh, they are such a waste of time."

My advice is to use networking events consistently as an entry point into a new industry; once you're established, ramp down the number of events you attend, perhaps focusing on a few that keep you connected.

Just use them as a survival technique initially. Remember, survival mode is intense, so plan to become an official organizer or leader of a Meetup group. My suggestion is not to start one, but to join one.

Networking events are useless for me now because I already know enough people to get connected to the people I want to. I'm already one or two connections away from Kevin Bacon.

(*Six Degrees of Kevin Bacon is a parlor game based on the "six degrees of separation" concept, which posits that any two people on earth are six or fewer acquaintance links apart. Movie buffs challenge each other to find the shortest path between an arbitrary actor and prolific character actor Kevin Bacon.*

The first major mistake most people make with networking is assuming that you have to know everyone. Is it good to know everyone? Sure. Is it possible? Absolutely not.)

Networking event tips:

- Do not go there with an agenda.
- Do not go there looking for a job.

The only real benefit of a networking event is when you start to see the same people over and over.

Here is how a conversation usually evolves if you attend the same event multiple times:

1st time: "Hi John, so what do you do?"

2nd time: "Hey John, good to see you again. How did your project end up?"

3rd time: "Hey John, it's a pleasure to see you as always. My project to get more connected in the digital marketing space has been going well. I'm looking to connect with the founders of digital marketing agencies in Chicago. What do you think the best avenue is for me to do this? Is there anyone that you can connect me with?"

Note: If you don't have a job right now and you're not creating anything, there's no reason why you aren't at these events at least three times a week. Going to a networking event is 100 times better than what you are doing now: "looking for jobs online."

Step 1.6: Get officially involved.

If you found a group you like, it's time to get involved in a low-commitment way so that it doesn't interfere with your job, but still gives back to the community and helps you maintain your edge. You never know how organizing an event or hosting a get-together of colleagues and acquaintances might benefit you.

Step 2: Take It To The Next Level: Expand Your Core Group And Become The Hub (Advanced)

Step 1 is a lot of work, I'll admit it. It works like hell, but yes, it's a lot of work.

You can complete this exercise even if you skip Step 1, but only if you already have a great core network. Professional networking is, in my opinion, the *act* of you becoming a professional at networking.

Whether you're a college student or a job seeker looking to advance, taking the grassroots approach to building a network pays off in huge dividends.

Let's say you have an excellent network of contacts and you want to build a closer relationship with your group and start involving influencers more often.

Start your own small networking group—a "hub" of sorts—by hosting a private, invite-only event around a niche topic or industry, either monthly or bi-monthly.

This is my recommended approach when it comes to building a hub. I would almost always start here:

1. Select 6-10 people in your industry that you have a good relationship with and ask them if they are open to meeting once a month or once a quarter. You can meet at a bar/restaurant to start it off. If you can meet at one of your offices, even better.

2. At the actual event, you can set a topic and discuss it. It doesn't need to be formal. You are opening your network to others, and you will now be helping your network be more connected.

3. The idea is that you keep expanding the group for each new event. You ask each member to refer one new person that you think would benefit from this group and help others.

What if you want to host a one-off private, invite-only dinner (or even breakfast)? Same concept as the private, invite-only groups, except this time, you invite new people every single time. This is much harder to pull off, in my opinion, but can reap a lot of great rewards.

And your guests will be aware of the value you're adding. Once, the host of a group charged $100 per event (dinner and drinks were included). It was a premium price to pay, but it brought in some great relationships. In other words, you can be creative with how you do this.

Step 3: Acquire The Tools And Processes To Maintain And Grow Your Network

Over a short period of time, I built one hell of a network. The problem soon became managing my network correctly. I use two tools to manage it. As you will quickly notice, they're nothing spectacular or out of the ordinary.

- LinkedIn
- Email or an email marketing tool such as MailChimp

Here's the process I use to manage a large group of people:

1. I make a new contact.
2. I add them on LinkedIn.

3. Send a quick email to them saying it was nice to meet them at the event.

4. In that email, I include this note: "I have an email newsletter that goes out about once a month. I help connect people in my network with each other and give them small updates about what I'm working on. Would you like to be added to it?"

5. Add them to my newsletter once they agree. This is where I use MailChimp.

6. Send out the newsletter once a month.

I do this consistently. No excuses.

Here's what I include in the newsletter:

Subject: *Robbie's connection newsletter #37*

Email Body:

Hi, all – Lots of great new things happening in my network this month. Here are some of the best ones.

Mark just launched a new company. You can check it out here <link>. If you like food, this is something to check out.

My good friend Jeff is looking for a new gig. He's the best project manager I know. You can find his resume here <link>.

Lisa is looking to hire a new marketing analyst. If that's you or someone you know, feel free to reach out to me and I'll connect you.

Lastly, this past month has been real busy for me. It doesn't feel like I got much done, but in reality I've done quite a bit! I'll be announcing it in a few months, once the project is ready to be launched.

That's all for this month!

As always, if you have anything to share with the group, please email me and I'll include it in the next newsletter.

This is all that I send, and it works wonders. I'm helping others get connected with one another, rendering me a "super connector" of sorts.

Also, if you didn't notice, I've essentially given myself job security. I now have a huge audience of people who can help me if I need to look for a job. Luckily, I haven't had to roll out that safety net, but it's nice knowing I have it.

I also use LinkedIn to post status updates and write new articles using LinkedIn Publisher. It keeps everyone in the loop about what I'm working on.

Step 4: Follow These General Networking Tips

Your network should consist of contacts, colleagues, references, mentors and protégés – and they should all be rooting for you.

People aren't computers: you can tick all the boxes on paper, but if they don't like you, they won't want to work with you, and they certainly won't go out of their way to help you.

1. Make it about them: Follow the 80/20 rule: Only 20% of a conversation should be about you. Listen to the person you're talking to instead of thinking about what they can do for you. Draw them out. Show a genuine interest. And if you can help them in any way, volunteer immediately.

While you are interested in selling your services, no one wants to feel like that's the only reason you're talking to them.

Furthermore, if you have taken an interest in their needs and goals, you'll be better situated to offer them services and suggestions you know they can use. If you can align your needs, you can benefit personally while working towards the greater good: there's nothing more attractive than a perfect fit.

2. Have integrity: It's about being trusted as much as it is being liked. Losing your reputation for honesty, fairness and straight dealing can be a deathblow: who's going to entrust you with anything important?

Be vulnerable: It's ok to ask for help or advice, and to be upfront about what you need. Trying to pussyfoot around the subject just makes you look shady. Telling people what you've tried, even if it hasn't worked, shows them that you're serious and already working on your own behalf. They may have tips and feedback to help you.

3. Be modest, but not too modest: Standing next to the big fish in your pond, you may feel rather small. But don't be intimidated – there's a fine line between paying your respects and pulling yourself down, and you need to draw it. This isn't the time to be modest: if you don't acknowledge your strengths, how is this highly connected stranger going to recognize them?

In the professional world, we like to think that status is a measure of merit. Rightly or wrongly so, we value confidence and competence, and being deferential implies that you're less capable than other people. No one's going to entrust you with a task you don't look like you can handle.

Even if you have fewer awards, a more limited reputation, and a weaker backhand in tennis, carry yourself as this person's equal. After all, you're not dying to work with the person who's a smaller fish than you, are you? Neither are they.

4. Discuss your side projects: You want to show that you're a hard worker, actively helping yourself instead of trying to ride on favors. No one likes a parasite, but it feels good to help someone who shows promise.

Side projects are great personal PR for two reasons: first, they're completely your baby, so they prove you're self-motivated and skilled enough to get shit done. Second, you can discuss them freely without giving the impression that you talk about your company's work out of school. Remember what I said about being trustworthy?

5. Respond: to that email or phone call. Keeping in touch with old friends is important.

6. Reconnect: Be the one to send the email or make the call, and catch up with old colleagues and companies.

7. Reach out: to new people. This is the tricky part, but don't let it intimidate you. There are ways and means of doing it effectively.

In conclusion, networking skills take work, but the payoffs are huge!

CHAPTER TEN

ONLINE NETWORKING 101

THERE IS A REASON I DON'T RECOMMEND THAT PEOPLE apply to jobs on other career-related sites. They are mostly a waste of time. LinkedIn, however, does it right.

It's the difference between "I can't find a job" and "I have several opportunities waiting for me."

It's that powerful.

If you treat it like the powerful platform it is, you will see significant growth in your career.

Every single job I have ever received is directly or indirectly related to my use and personal branding on LinkedIn. Because I took the time to learn how to use LinkedIn, I went from 500 connections to 30,000 connections (or followers) in three months. I'll share my strategy. Less fluff, and more how-to.

Your LinkedIn profile sucks. Trust me. I've seen thousands of them. Additionally, there is a 99% chance after reading this guide, you won't take any action, and continue to suck at LinkedIn.

Can't you tell that I'm an optimist?

For the 1% who are going to take action, keep reading!

Step 1: You need to pay for a professional LinkedIn profile picture. No, seriously.

I honestly don't recommend paying for many things. A professional picture is on the top of my list of things to pay for. Your selfie isn't going to work. That great picture of you that your buddy snapped before you went out on a night of town, isn't going to work. If you didn't pay for it, there is a 99.99% chance the picture shouldn't be your profile picture.

It's the difference between "I want to learn more about this person" and "I have no interest in this person...Next!"

Keep in mind that once you've paid for a great headshot, you can reuse it for your own personal blog or publications, for any other online professional representation of you, and your personal brand.

Your perfect profile picture should tick the following boxes:

- Great lighting.
- Awesome resolution.
- A simple background.
- Full, glorious color.
- A neat, head-and-shoulders photograph of your face.

What should you do while you're saving up the $150-$250 to pay a photographer who's done this kind of thing before? There are few photos that are worse than having no photo at all, but they do exist and you've probably seen at least one of these examples.

In the interim, try to stick to these simple guidelines for any profile picture you use, and use the following factors to check your final image again for "psychological satisfaction" before you hit "upload."

Long story short, you need a great picture. It's seriously a world of a difference. Don't ignore this.

Step 2: Write a summary statement that is accurate AND interesting.

Ok, now that I'm done yelling at you for having a bad photo, let's talk about your summary statement in LinkedIn.

"Robbie is an innovative marketing professional with over 15 years' experience in the industry..."

Are you bored yet? I am, and that sentence is all about me.

LinkedIn gives you 2,000 characters to provide a comprehensive window into who you are and what makes you tick—not just as an employee, but also as a person. I mean, a 2,000-character-long bio on the Internet is just a step below a full memoir. Am I right?

Your summary needs to sell you, but it needs to do it authentically. Start at the beginning. Share your values. Have a sense of humor. Be a real, living, breathing person with goals, ambitions, fears, interests, skills and hobbies. After reading your summary, your viewers should feel like they've just met you for a friendly chat over a cup of coffee.

Your summary should cover the five bases:

1. Value statement. This should be your very first sentence, and you'd better make it good. You don't have to focus on what you're

currently doing: the point is to tell the reader exactly what they'd get out of working with you.

I help companies create content that people actually want to read.

I also help miserable people see the light in their career.

2. *Why* you do what you do. Now that you've got their attention, use a couple of paragraphs to tell your story. Where have you been? What do you stand for? Where do you want to go? Use stories and anecdotes to keep things human and engaging.

Transitioning from IT to Digital Marketing & Career Advancement was one of the toughest transitions of my life.

I went through a life crisis trying it figure it all out. Going through a life and identity crisis while your bank account also depends on the answer is something I hope you never have to go through.

I went from being an expert in "IT Consulting" with nine years experience to becoming a "Marketing Director" and "Career Advancement Expert" within two years. I not only destroyed the ceiling that was preventing me from advancing but positioned myself never to have a ceiling control my career and my life. I have never felt this free in my entire life.

My goal is to help you learn from my mistakes.

3. Interesting facts. This is the main advantage of LinkedIn over a traditional resume: you can tell the reader anything you think they need to know. Perhaps you have expertise that isn't covered by your qualifications, or want to branch out in a direction where you have no formal experience. This is the place for things that don't fit inside a bullet-point list.

I wrote the book conservatively titled, "Fire Me I Beg You."

LinkedIn chose one of my posts as one of the best articles in 2014.

My articles have accumulated over 3 million views with four posts over 400,000 views.

I built a strong professional network in Chicago with growing startups, investors & successful entrepreneurs by taking 250 coffee meetings in 400 days.

The CEO of Deloitte Consulting loved my resignation letter so much; he sent it to the entire company.He is now the CEO of Deloitte Global.

My writing has been featured in the New York Times, Business Insider, Forbes, CBS News and Lifehacker.

I stalked James Altucher for four years, and the result was him inviting me to participate in his award-winning podcast.

I built an email list of 10,000 people in 5 months using LinkedIn.

4. How you can help me. Time to lay it on the line. This section isn't just about telling the reader what you can do, but emphasizes that you're willing to do it for them. You need to let them have the Holy Grail: give out your email address.

I include the line: "Email me at robbie@firemeibegyou.com. I read every email."

That last little statement says two things: that you get a lot of emails, and that you make time for the people who send them to you.

5. Special skills. This section plays two parts: First, telling people what you do. Second, providing terms that will show up in keyword searches.

Ghostwriter, digital marketer, career coach, speaker.

Step 3: Use the "Media" section.

This is why a LinkedIn profile pays 10x more than a resume. Give some life to your profile.

Step 4: You need to fill in all of the fields, unfortunately.

This is a no-brainer, but it's an important one. According to an article by Link Humans, "Your profile is 15 times more likely to be viewed by adding the industry you work in and ten times more likely to be viewed if you add your education." But that doesn't mean filling in each field with stream-of-consciousness, buzzword heavy nonsense will cut it.

Step 5: Fill out your job history. Include descriptions for each position – in the first person!

Do not, I repeat, *do not* import your resume straight into LinkedIn. Yes, the option exists. But the option to buy and then eat thumbtacks also exists, and you don't need to be told not to do that. Do you?

Hiring managers want to see that you're a great fit for a role, so use your past career steps as chapters in the story of you. Make it clear to them that hiring you is the only logical way for the story to continue. This is another test your one-sentence story has to pass. Does your experience at Wing Pit in college fit into the narrative as a Director of Marketing? You decide.

Step 6: Ditch the buzzwords. You're not a "motivated team player." Trust me, no one believes you.

Truly innovative people don't say that they're "innovative"... because they're too busy innovating. Let your accomplishments do the talking for you, and try to avoid coming across as a repetitive corporate robot. Hint: If the word "synergy" appears in your summary in a non-ironic way, think about rewriting. Just saying.

Step 7: Stick to the first person.

Instead of saying "Robbie is an experienced project management professional," you can say something along the lines of "I have worked in many Fortune 500 companies as a project manager. My specific focus is SAP software implementations."

If you're not used to blowing your own horn, it's time to sign up for trumpet lessons. Using the third person makes it sound like you've got some kind of dissociative disorder, or that you're trying to make it sound like your profile summary came from someone else. The only items that should sound like they came from someone else are the glowing referrals on your profile. More about those later.

Step 8: Think twice about any qualifications in your title.

I had my project management certification and the qualification was a "PMP." So I put my name as Robbie Abed, PMP. Long story short, I got more inMails from my friends telling me that I'm missing the "I" in PMP than I actually got from qualified leads.

I also realized that many hiring managers viewed a Project Management Certification as a nice to have and not a must have.

Unless the job you want specifically requires a qualification (like a Medical Doctor), it's probably not that relevant to any recruiters looking to hire, and it might actually pigeonhole you and limit your potential reach. If you've got your diploma in journalism, but want to get into B2B communications, chances are that 'Dip.' abbreviation at the end of your name will make your profile views do just that—dip.

Step 9: You might also want to reconsider naming the company you work for in your subtitle.

Similarly, if you're holding down a position at a well-known or particularly credible company, then you might do well to include the name in your title.

But bear in mind that just saying "Director of Sales" sounds more impressive than "Director of Sales at Mrs. Tinsley's Instant Soup Factory." Remember, dress for the job you want.

Step 10: You might even want to rethink your own name. Especially if your name is John Smith.

If your name is John Smith, you're screwed. You would literally have to find the cure to cancer, win an NFL championship and the Tour De France to even be considered for the first result for your name search on Google or LinkedIn.

If and when you Google yourself, if your name isn't as unique as you thought it was, it's time to start differentiating yourself. If you have a second name or the option of a double-barrel surname, start adding that to your online profiles. "James Johnson" might not be memorable on its own, but add that second name your parents thoughtfully added to your birth certificate and now, Mr. James Peter Johnson, you've got a much better chance of being found online.

Disclaimer: I'm not recommending you drop your last name, like Adele, Prince or Rihanna. Nor do I think this is the ideal opportunity to use that great nickname you got in 5th grade.

The key is to then use that same name across every online channel. Your email signature, LinkedIn, Facebook, etc.

Step 11: Use the "City" field strategically when looking for jobs in a place you don't yet live.

The "city" field seems like an obvious one to get right. You just enter the city that you're currently living and working in, right? Not so much. Let's say you're based in Fort Lauderdale, but have dreams of moving to New York. You'd up and move if only the right career opportunity came along. But how is that opportunity going to come along when all of New York's hiring managers are striking you off their list because it looks like you're happy where you are? Correct their assumption.

List the city you want to work in to start getting noticed by recruiters in this area, so you can make sure you show in their searches.

I'm not saying lie about your current location. Don't lie about where your current job is. Tell the truth, but you can put the city you want to work in and be kosher in my book.

Step 12: Start showing up higher on LinkedIn searches.

You don't need to stuff your profile full of keywords to rank highly on LinkedIn. That kind of thing might just drive a potential hiring manager or partner nuts before they've even gotten as far as your email address.

Making sure that people looking for you can find you *does* mean making sure that your profile has been optimized to appear in the right searches. Check that your job titles, descriptions, summary and even your recommendations are all telling the same story.

Part 2: Amplify your voice by publishing articles into the online void (no, writing isn't too hard).

It takes a reader a fraction of a second to get that precious first impression, and at best a couple of minutes to read your whole profile. That's as long as you've got to make an impact – or is it?

LinkedIn's publishing platform may be its most undervalued tool. It gives you access to a broader audience for longer periods of time. People will come to hear what you have to say, and if it resonates, they'll want to hear more. That's how relationships start.

Writing and distributing articles using LinkedIn publishing is a great way to turn browsers into followers and followers into connections. My results haven't been too shabby, if I do say so myself. For instance, after 120 days of article writing on LinkedIn, I'd achieved:

- 1.6 Million Article Views
- 50 new high-quality relationships added to "Robbie's Connection Newsletter"
- 7,500 email subscribers added to my email list
- 10,447 new followers (Yes, LinkedIn has followers, which are separate from connections)
- 1,100 new connections

I also learned a few things along the way – these days I refer to the following checklist before I post an article. I found a score of 7 or more is a pretty good sign it will be a success:

- Makes reader feel inspired / motivated: **+4**
- Agreeable tone / content: **+4**
- Authentic first-person story: **+3**
- Recent events in technology / business: **+3**
- Topic: Career Advancement / Leadership: **+2**
- Actionable tips / lessons learned: **+1**
- Industry-specific / technical*: **-2**
- Clickbait headline: **-3**

SECTION THREE: THE TRADITIONAL ROUTE

CHAPTER ELEVEN

YOUR PATH MAY VARY

ALL OF THE ASPECTS OF SURVIVAL MODE BUILD UP TO THIS one question: How do I make money doing this?

You have two routes:

1) The traditional route: Become a full-time employee

2) The non-traditional route: Hustle and entrepreneurship

Neither option is more honorable than the other.

Neither do I think these options are mutually exclusive. In fact, most successful entrepreneurs do both.

What the future holds for you is unknown, but you should have an idea of what some outcomes are. Here are some realistic paths.

Quit. Explore; network. Find another full-time job in a different industry.

Quit. Explore; network. Find another full-time job in the same industry.

Quit. Start a new company. Fail. Find another full-time job.

Quit. Start a new company. Succeed. Then ultimately fail. Find another full-time job.

Quit. Join a startup. You hate it. You go back to your old job.

Quit. Start a new company. Succeed. Sell the company. Become rich. Start another company.

Quit. Explore; network. Struggle. Mid-life crisis. Survive. Find another job.

Quit, Explore; network. Struggle. Mid-life crisis. Survive. Become a freelancer.

Quit. Mid-life crisis. Depression. Move back in with parents.

Quit. Midlife crisis. Depression. Become an artist. Actually get paid for being an artist.

Quit. Midlife crisis. Depression. Become an artist. Figure out you're actually not a good artist. Or maybe just not a lucrative one? Find part-time work. Find a full-time job.

Don't quit. Stay miserable. Get laid off. Find another full-time job.

Don't quit. Stay miserable. Never get laid off. Stay miserable.

Quit. Start a new company. Fail. Get another job. Quit. Start a new company. Fail. Get another job. Quit. Start a new company. Survive. Succeed.

Quit. Explore; network. Meet a girl who says she wants to bring you with her to Indonesia from San Francisco. You're ecstatic. The day before she texts you that she can't go anymore. Still go anyway. Glad she wasn't able to come with you. Find another job working remotely from anywhere in the world.

YOU GET THE POINT.

There are a million paths that you can take. None of the options will be clear to you when you quit.

And yes, the last scenario is a true story. Not my story, but from a good friend of mine.

Your Path May Vary (YPMV)

Let's focus on how to make your path a success in the end.

CHAPTER TWELVE

REPLACE YOUR AWFUL JOB WITH A BETTER ONE

You may be reading this book with zero intention of becoming an entrepreneur. That's ok.

You just need to be the best at what you do. Not just good, but the best.

What's interesting about most career advice I see online is that nobody ever talks about what matters most: how good you are at your job. All the interview tips in the world won't work if it's clear you aren't good at what you do.

Being good at what you do is the best personal branding you can ever do for yourself. People don't want to market themselves, but by being great at what you do, you market yourself every day.

So, how do you become the best at what you do?

Become A Double Threat

I stole this term from Neville Medhora who wrote a great article titled "The Most Successful People Are a Double Threat (or More)."

Here's a excerpt blatantly stolen from Neville's article. It's that good.

Single Threat = Knows a skill. Value = $

Double Threat = Knows a skill + another useful skill. Value = $$

Triple Threat = Knows a skill + another useful skill + yet another useful skill. Value = $$$$$

For example, I'm a writer + marketer + technologist. This means that I can write great content, know how to market it, and be able to use the right platforms online to see my content gets distributed far and wide.

For the most part, all of these skills are self-taught. But can you see the advantage I have over someone who is just a writer? I can also use these skill sets to get an executive position as, say, Director of Marketing by combining content, marketing and technology. I'll beat out any traditional marketer any day of the week.

So how do you become a double threat?

You don't become a double threat by learning on the job. You're going to learn off the job.

The best way to do this is to create a side hustle (AKA a passion project) with full knowledge that your side hustle will most likely never replace your current job.

You NEED a side hustle. A side hustle almost always requires a skill that you don't have. It requires an ability to market yourself or your product. It requires technical knowledge to build components of your business. It requires a network of people that can help you market your business or refer you leads. It requires a Rolodex of contractors that can help you with things you just can't do for yourself. It requires you to face failure every single day. It requires you to understand a market better than you ever thought imaginable.

Most importantly, it forces you to learn.

Fire Me I Beg You was a side hustle.

The reason I'm so good at marketing now is because of the first version of *Fire Me I Beg You*. I wrote 200 articles in one year. I became a better writer because of it. When I released my book, I had no idea how to market it. One year later, I was coaching others on how to become better at marketing.

It forced me to become a better writer and marketer. I would have never learned this at my full-time IT job.

I think I did OK for myself.

Side hustles are how you become the best at what you do. They're how you complement your primary job. Instead of being a great accountant that only a few people within your company know about, you're now a great accountant with an excellent website, network and social media chops that help you land your next higher-paying job and some side income.

You must get out of your brain that the full-time company you work for is responsible for making you better at what you do. I'll give you more detailed instructions on how to launch a side hustle later in this book.

There are two more things that you need to do to truly become the best at what you do.

Tell The World Exactly What You're Good At

It all starts with you knowing what you're good at. This is how you do it:

Tell the story of your life.

Think of the last four people you recently met for the first time. Now write down what their story was in one sentence. For example, here are a few people I met at an event in Chicago:

1. A guy with two or three side projects and a full-time job at a big company.
2. A bright strategy consultant who believes digital is the only place to be. She has no digital experience, but is looking to connect with digital agencies in Chicago with hopes to join a growing company.
3. Someone who enjoys entrepreneurship and wants to learn more.
4. Someone looking for a new IT job.

Of these four people, which one do you think has the best story?

Let me rephrase that. Which one of these people do you think has the simplest and most clearly understood story?

For me, #2 has the best story. During the four minutes I talked to this person I knew:

- What her job currently is in very clear terms.
- What job she is pursuing.
- Where she needs help (connecting with digital agencies).

Of those four people, she is the only one I keep in touch with. I've helped her achieve her goal of connecting with digital agencies in Chicago. The most important part of her story was that I could understand it, and I could clearly understand how I could help her achieve her next goal.

I already forgot almost everything about the other three.

I remembered the bright strategy consultant because I felt something as she told her story. You see, her story was all about the *why*. The other three were all about *what*. This is the fundamental mistake amateur storytellers make.

They drop loads of forgettable details, but never get to the essence that is the why. As in, why is this important to you? Why should it be important to me? An honest story is inspiring, always.

I want you to write down what your one-sentence story is. This story is focused on your current skill set. The next step is to create one focused on your future skill set.

I'll show you how I came up with my own story. The key is that I don't know what the end result will be; I just type what first comes to my mind. I press enter, and I do it again and again until I've discovered the reason why, not just the what or the how.

Here is an unedited flow of how I came up with my story in 2012.

- I'm an IT Consultant.
- I help clients help themselves.
- I'm an IT Project Manager who leads complex IT projects.
- I'm a self-taught developer who manages IT projects.
- I lead complex IT projects as an independent consultant, specializing in SAP Software.
- I'm a technical Project Manager who leads IT projects for enterprise companies.
- I help deliver projects through my communication skills.

- I'm a Project Manager whose main focus is to manage IT projects.
- My goal is to make everyone's life easier through leading complex IT projects.
- My mission is to make your life easier by helping solve complex IT issues and projects.
- I will make your life easier by untangling and delivering your complex IT projects.
- I solve complex IT problems while making everyone's life easier.
- IT projects all have the same problem regardless of what the technology is. My specialty is untangling troubled IT projects with clear guidance from IT and Business.
- My specialty is untangling complex IT projects by acting as a communication bridge between IT and Business.
- My specialty is turning around and leading complex IT projects by acting as a communications bridge between IT and Business.
- I lead complex IT projects because I believe IT has power, but if it's not supported with great communications, nobody knows what to do.
- I believe in the power of IT. My specialty is turning around and leading complex IT projects.

Ah, yes! This last one sounds great for me.

If someone asks me who I am/what I do in conversation, my answer is "I believe in the power of IT. My specialty is turning around and leading complex IT projects."

That's my current story. The other stories were good, but they weren't clear enough and they weren't powerful enough. Let's be honest—we're not going to remember your details, but we will remember what you stood for.

Now let's move on to your future story. Ideally, your future story is what you will be known for if everything works out the way you planned it.

Here's my unedited flow of how I came up with my future story while I was writing *Fire Me I Beg You*.

- I'm an IT Career Coach.
- I help IT professionals advance their careers.
- I mentor business professionals looking to advance their careers.
- I empower business professionals to take ownership of their own careers.
- I help motivated business professionals transition to self-employment.
- I mentor business professionals who were recently laid off.
- I mentor business professionals who are interested in transitioning into a career in digital marketing.
- I mentor business professionals on how to transform from being a consumer to becoming a creator.
- I mentor technology professionals who have built successful careers in the enterprise space and are interested in entrepreneurship.
- I help successful business professionals transform their careers into entrepreneurship.
- I specialize in helping successful IT workers build a career in a non-IT field.
- I believe in mentoring recently laid off business and IT professionals who are looking to re-invent their careers as entrepreneurs.

- I help IT professionals re-invent their career

The key concept to understand here is that my future story will change almost weekly, as I develop myself and my skills. It will continue to evolve naturally.

But the essential foundation will never change. At the heart of it, I believe in helping people. Regardless of how it manifests itself, the "why" never changes. Sure, the "what" I do may change over time, but the reason I do the things I do–that remains constant.

The first story will help you make money now.

The second story will help you make money in the future.

Use the first story until it makes sense to transition to the second story.

Show Undeniable Proof (AKA "Social Proof") That You're The Best At What You Do

When someone tells me that they are great at something—say, Instagram marketing—the first thing I do is look at their Instagram profile or their company's Instagram. If they have less than 100 followers, then something is off. In this instance, they don't have social proof and it's an immediate turn-off.

The same applies to you. These days, employers don't want to know where you've worked or what your duties were. They want to see your work.

- If you're a programmer, they'll ask you to show them what you've created.
- If you're an editor, they'll ask you to show them the before and after of an article you've edited.

- If you're a marketer, they'll ask you to show them a marketing plan you've created and the results it got.
- If you're a designer, they'll ask you to show them your portfolio.
- If you're an accountant, they'll ask you to show them what you did to help people save thousands of dollars on their tax returns every year.
- If you're a lawyer, they'll ask you to show them what laws are working against them and how you can better structure their company to avoid such things.

Show employers that you know what you're talking about – that's the main deliverable potential employers are asking for today. It also happens to be the core problem with resumes. They're all about telling and not showing.

Many times you won't be able to show your work because it's for a client or your company, and you can't go around sharing presentations, designs or excel sheets with the whole world. How do you get around showing your talent when you can't share any of your work because of company confidentiality reasons?

Write about your experiences on LinkedIn or Medium, and don't mention client names or the company you work for. Teach the world something new from your angle. You can then include these links in your email signature.

Side note: This is why it's important to have a side hustle. That way you have a little bit more control over how you show your work.

CHAPTER THIRTEEN

EVERYTHING YOU NEED TO KNOW ABOUT FINDING A JOB

FINDING A NEW JOB ISN'T LIKE IT USED TO BE. THE PROCESS back then was strictly limited to the following rubric: create your resume, apply online, get interviews.

Now when you apply for a job online, you'll be lucky if you ever get a response. Hell, most people would celebrate getting an acknowledgment email.

This old process is a good recipe for spiraling into a deep, unproductive depression. The good news is that I have a solution. And it works. Let's focus on what works, shall we?

The 10 Commandments Of Finding A New Job

1. The hidden job market is real. Most jobs waiting to be filled are not posted online. Just because you don't see a job listing doesn't mean the company isn't hiring. Get that out of your head right now. Don't get discouraged if you don't see a job posting regarding a position you want, or with a company you want to work at.

2. It's not about who you know. It's all about knowing the right people who know that you're good at what you do. Read those two sentences again. I know plenty of extremely well-connected people who for the life of them can't advance their career because they haven't grasped this lesson. You need to fill your network with people who have a clear idea of what you do and who you are (and what you can do for them).

3. Applying for a job online is the worst way to go about it. Even if you don't know anyone who works at your target company, submitting your resume cold turkey through an online site is always a terrible idea. This is especially applicable when the job you're at isn't an exact match for the job you are applying for. There's a better way to do this, and I'll show you.

4. The resume is dead. If you spend an hour a year on your resume, that's more than enough. I will admit that the resume is still needed for formality's sake. However, LinkedIn should be your new focus, and your most up-to-date, online resume replacement.

5. You don't need a formal education to do your job. Unless you're a doctor, lawyer, scientist or in another profession that requires a certain advanced degree, you do not need a formal education. There are any number of successful business entrepreneurs who are thriving without a degree. All you need is a little determination and the Internet. The Internet is an amazing place. Use it to your advantage.

6. People hire people. Don't be afraid of reaching out to people more successful than you. Nobody is doing you a favor by hiring you. They will hire you if they think you can make their lives easier. You make their lives easier by doing good work. Successful people want to hire other successful people.

7. Companies don't hire you because they like you. They hire you for a very selfish reason. They want to make more money! Hiring you enables them to save more money or make more money. You are there to help them achieve that goal. The better you position yourself to help them make more money or save more money, the easier your job search will become.

8. Nobody will hire you for someone you want to be (except for your mother or your uncle). Companies need help from someone who has proven experience and knows what they're doing. They don't care where you see yourself five years from now. They might ask you that question during an interview, but trust me, they don't give a shit. This is probably the hardest pill to swallow for many of you. How do you get a new job if you can't get the experience the new job requires? This brings me to...

9. Switching careers is never a straight line. If you want to go from IT to Marketing, don't expect to just jump from one job to another. This applies to any career where you don't have relevant professional experience. In reality, a lot of things happen in the middle of a "career transition" that lead up to your successful arrival. Nobody will hire you as a marketer when all of your experience is in IT. To change careers without starting all over, you must launch a side hustle, which I'll explain more about below.

10. If your first contact for a job is an online job application, a recruiter, or Human Resources, you're doing it wrong. I don't have any issues with HR or recruiters. They are needed. Except that they are the gatekeepers and almost never make the final decision. What I found funny is that for my last two jobs, on paper, I was unqualified for the job. If I went through HR or a job application, I would have never received an initial interview. What I did differently for these jobs is that I got support from the

VPs *before* applying. Since I had that endorsement, it made the entire process much smoother. I didn't have to prove myself. I didn't have to answer "where I see myself in five years."

These questions were already answered prior to my first interview, and the rest of the interviews were focused on what the role demanded and how I could help contribute. If you want to learn more about how to bypass gatekeepers, go to FireMeIBegYou.com.

These ten commandments are important to remember, but none of these commandments are helpful if you don't take action. Luckily for you, I created a section dedicated to helping you identify where to start. I call this part, "Now What?"

But first, I recognize that this can be a lot to swallow. So, stop slouching, get up, stretch and observe your surroundings. Find something around you that you appreciate and recognize its existence. Take a few minutes' break before starting this new section.

Now What?

Done stretching? Great. Let's take the ten commandments and condense them into five simple steps.

Step #1 – Be the best at what you do.

Step #2 – Tell the world exactly what you're good at.

Step #3 – Show undeniable proof that you're the best at what you do.

Step #4 – Bypass the traditional hiring system by building direct relationships with executives.

Step #5 – Become better at what you do, even if you're already the best.

When you nail these five steps, you won't find yourself looking for jobs. You won't be looking because you will be getting job offers, constantly. It's amazing how many opportunities present themselves once people know what it is you do (and that you do it well!)

CHAPTER FOURTEEN

HOW TO NAIL ANY INTERVIEW

WHETHER YOU'RE PLANNING ON WORKING FOR YOURSELF--with no intention of interviewing for any position in the near future--or you're looking for a new job immediately, knowing how to interview is one of the easiest life skills to master with some of the most outsized results. In this chapter, I'll teach you to avoid all the painful and costly errors I've made.

I was once the world's worst job interviewee. You name it; I made the mistake.

I called interviewers by the wrong name.

I told interviewers that I didn't appreciate that my paid-for flight had a connection and whoever organized my hotel was not an organized person. (I still cringe thinking about this one. I didn't get the job, and I can pinpoint it to this exact moment.)

I name-dropped people the interviewers didn't get along with.

I opened up my Dell laptop while I was waiting for my interview at IBM Headquarters (when IBM was in the computer business and a direct competitor to Dell).

I arrived late to interviews because I went to the wrong office.

I screwed myself out of thousands of dollars during salary negotiation because of things I said during my interview. This unfortunately happened multiple times.

I had 17 interviews with Google. 17! I kid you not. This was for one job. I messed it up at the end by talking smack about a bad boss. To be fair, the question was "Tell me about your worst manager." I fell for it, and I'm 99% certain I lost the job because of the way I answered it.

I took phone interviews while I was half asleep during the middle of the day. (This was for Google attempt #2. I still lose sleep over how stupid I was to pick up the phone after I was taking a midday nap, AND THEN PROCEEDED TO TAKE THE INTERVIEW.)

The good news is that I'm alive and I'm here to tell you everything I know about interviewing.

I'm going to teach you how to flip the script and have a competitive advantage before your first interview is even conducted. In flipping the script and learning my new interview skills and techniques, you can significantly improve your odds of getting what you want, and avoid cringe-worthy mistakes that will haunt you.

If it works for me, it can work for you. Ready?

Change your mindset. Everything you know about interviewing is wrong.

The actual interview doesn't happen during the interview.

It happens before the interview begins. Before the first HR phone interview. Before the first on-site interviews. It happens even before you get the first email inviting you to interview.

Read this little quip from the former SVP of People at Google:

In other words, most interviews are a waste of time because 99.4 percent of the time is spent trying to confirm whatever impression the interviewer formed in the first ten seconds. "Tell me about yourself." "What is your greatest weakness?" "What is your greatest strength?" Worthless.

If you're like me, you're probably the worst first-impression-maker of all time.

So, if 99.4% of the time, the interview is a waste of time because they are too busy confirming their bias, what do you do? You make the first impression before you speak to them.

Remember the five steps from the last chapter?

Step #1 – Be the best at what you do.

Step #2 – Tell the world exactly what you're good at.

Step #3 – Show undeniable proof that you're the best at what you do.

Step #4 – Bypass the traditional hiring system by building direct relationships with executives.

Step #5 – Become better at what you do, even if you're already the best.

If you did steps #1 – 5 correctly, interviewing should be a breeze. How you got the interview is 10 times more important than the interview itself.

Let me lay out a real-life example. I received a random Facebook message from a college friend. Their company was hiring, and she thought I would be a great fit. She introduced me to the SVP of the division.

I had one somewhat formal phone interview, and he invited me to attend the once-a-year company party and also speak with the other people in the division.

I was the only person invited to the party who didn't work at the company. The people I had interviewed with the day before the company were astonished that I was invited to the event. "How did you get invited to the company party? You don't even work here yet? I'm not even sure why I'm interviewing you."

I still remember when one of my interviewers told this to me. I had the job in the bag *before* the formal interviews even began. All I needed was the SVP to give his blessing, and the rest was downhill. Keep in mind, HR and Recruiting had no idea I even exist. I submitted my resume as a formality after our interviews were complete.

I proceeded to have a blast and meet everyone I would potentially work with at the party.

Now, I'm not telling you this to brag. I'm telling you this so you understand that you don't have to follow the traditional hiring system to go through the process. The faster you can get an SVP to endorse you for a job, the better everything comes.

So, How Did I Get An Endorsement From An SVP Before Formal Interviews Even Began? Or: How To Get A Competitive Edge Before The Interview Starts

I wrote an article about productivity and project management. My friend, whom I hadn't spoken to in four years, loved my post and thought I would be a good fit for their growing company. She also had a great relationship with the SVP.

I told her I was happy where I was, but I would be interested in learning more.

The productivity post had over 400,000 views, and that was amazing social proof

that I knew what I was doing. That's all the SVP needed to hear. Our phone interview was less than 15 minutes before he invited me to the company party.

Social Proof Makes Every Interview A Breeze

I never got asked, "What's your greatest strength?" You know why? They already knew what my greatest strength was. They already read my article on productivity and project management. They saw all the comments on the article. They already read my LinkedIn profile, which laid out clearly why someone would hire me.

So, when I walked into my first formal on-site interview, it was immediately a conversation. The SVP already told the interviewers that he liked me. The deal was done before I arrived.

What does this mean for you?

This means that you have to work on building social proof and making sure your online presence tells everyone what you're good at. If the interviewers don't know anything about you during your first interview, you lost. You made your life that much more challenging.

Before you walk into an interview, the interviewer has gotten as much information about you as possible. Not just your resume. Also your LinkedIn profile, social media, and Google.

Let that sink in. Before you even utter a word to a real person, they have already formed a judgment of you. You're interviewing with real humans, after all. This is human nature. Now take advantage of this knowledge.

I know what you're thinking. But, Robbie, this is why I created a resume! My resume tells the interviewers everything important about me!

A resume is a factual representation of your professional experience. It doesn't allow links to your other work. It doesn't actually allow you to craft a story of who you are and what your work represents to you. It doesn't allow people to endorse you, or respond to your work. It's not a good storytelling mechanism. You need to tell a great story.

Here's a bonus list of social proof that could apply to any position:

- Being mentioned in an article by a business magazine such as Inc., *Forbes, Fortune, Huffington Post*, etc.
- Getting more than 10 comments on a blog post you wrote.
- Getting more than 10,000 views on a YouTube video you created.
- Being the speaker or panelist at a well-known conference.
- Getting more than 20 recommendations on your LinkedIn profile.

Ironically, having an excellent LinkedIn profile and having social proof are the biggest factors in both getting an interview and nailing it.

Before, During and After.

That's it! You're all done!

You're probably thinking: Robbie, I don't believe that Google guy who says 99.4% of interview decisions are made within the first 10 seconds. Give me the details of how to nail an interview. Don't BS me.

Ok, ok. Do you still want to prepare for the .6%? Let's do it.

Step 1: Research

Got an interview? Congratulations. Now, let's make sure you close the deal. The next step is to tell your interviewer everything they want to hear—without lying or stretching the truth.

I don't recommend lying– ever. Lying is not an option. You want to focus on forming the ideas they will take away from meeting you within those precious first 10 seconds.

The problem with this is figuring out what they're looking for. Each interviewer has their own agenda. You might interview with three people in the same department for a position, but all three interviewers likely have different reasons for interviewing you. Maybe Jane is too busy and wants to offload some of her workload to you. Ryan needs your help leading a new marketing initiative, similar to what you did at a previous employer. Frank didn't like the first person that worked there and just wants to make sure you can get along with people in the office.

If you were lucky enough to know this information beforehand, you would modify your message in each interview.

Jane's interview: You would emphasize your ability to get things done with minimal supervision.

Ryan's interview: You would talk about the results from the last marketing project and the process you undertook to make it a success.

Frank's interview: You would emphasize your ability to get along with others and provide examples of how your friendships have helped the company grow.

There's just one small problem. How do you get inside the interviewer's head before the interview starts? Ahhh yes, never fear— Robbie is here.

Research The Company

Use social media to get to know everything humanly possible about the company you're interviewing with. If you know who is going to interview you, you get bonus points.

Here are some things I do when researching companies:

- I look up their company name on LinkedIn to see how many employees they have.
- I use LinkedIn to see how many employees at the prospective employer have my job title or a similar title. Am I going to be 1 of 100, or am I going to be the only one with this job title?
- I look for recent news on the company. I do this by going to Google News and searching for the company name to see what comes up. Use quotes when searching the company name to make sure only exact results appear.
- I look on Twitter to see if they've posted any news that doesn't show up on their site.
- I research the interviewer.

You won't always have this information, but if you do, that's a bonus for you.

If possible, I usually ask HR or my first contact within the company about who exactly will be interviewing me.

I'll say something like "Is it possible to get the full name of the person interviewing me tomorrow? This information helps me prepare for the interview and make sure it's productive for both of us. Thank you!"

If that doesn't work, I'll use Advanced Search on LinkedIn and search for "HR" or "Product Manager" with the company name as a filter to narrow down who I might be talking to.

Once you know the name of the person you're interviewing with, look them up on Google, LinkedIn, Twitter, Facebook and any other social media platforms. Your goal is to understand more about them so you can customize your answers based on what they want to hear.

Let me repeat this again: The key to a successful interview is telling the interviewer exactly what they want to hear. They're asking you questions not because they don't know the answers, but because they want to hear your take on them. They already know what a good answer is. The more you know about them, the more you can understand what answers they will like or dislike.

For example, they might have tweeted or written an article on LinkedIn about how they don't think MBAs are worth the investment. Now you know not to say things like "Well, I learned this in one of my MBA classes at blah blah University." This information from stalking helps tremendously. So stalk away, my friends.

No blackmail. Just legal, professional, informational-gathering stalking!

Use Any Of Your Connections To Get the Inside Scoop

Go on LinkedIn and search for anyone that has worked at the company or still works at the company where you're applying.

If you've been a good job searcher, you've been keeping strong relationships with your LinkedIn contacts. Reach out to them and tell them you have an interview coming up and you would love to ask them a few questions.

People are more open to helping you than you think. They'll also provide more information that can be helpful when it comes to interviewing.

STEP 2: Pre-suasion

You know how OJ Simpson got away with murder? His lawyers told a better story than the prosecutors.

What I'm saying is that your story matters more than you think. Your story has to be more than a list of facts, which is basically your resume.

Telling a story is scientifically proven to activate our brains. If you're an Android user and can't fathom for the life of you why everyone loves Apple so much, then I'm talking especially to you.

LinkedIn is the center of your online brand. You should do everything in your power to get them to look at your LinkedIn profile, assuming it's up to date and you followed my comprehensive LinkedIn guide, plus any published articles of yours.

If you do this properly, you will find the rest of the interviews to be dramatically easier and more productive.

STEP 3: Flip The Script

OK, you've got your story down. You've got enough information about the employer and interviewers. Now comes the actual interview.

I'm going to assume you look good, smell good and have extra copies of your resume (that match your LinkedIn profile, of course) with you. You have to make another small—but mighty—mental change. This company is hiring you so you can teach them something, not the other way around.

I only learned this trick after becoming an independent consultant. The rules are different when you're an independent consultant. The expectations were clear from each employer. I realized that they weren't hiring me so they could train me to grow into a role. They were hiring me because they needed my help with something specific. If I didn't know exactly how to do it, they weren't going to hire me.

That's the change you have to make. You're approaching this interviewer with a proven track record of you being able to do what they need you to do. The new goal: They talk. You listen. You should know how to handle the basic interview questions, but ideally, you want the interviewer to spend more time telling you about the job than grilling you.

But first...

Establish credibility with real stories from your career as early as possible in the interview. I don't want to be grilled with hard questions for 30 minutes. I want to establish credibility right away, so I can spend the rest of the time grilling them. This is the core of "flipping the script." Let's turn the tables on them.

I establish credibility by telling very candid and specific stories about how I achieved a goal that's relevant to the reason I'm being hired. For example, I was interviewing for a project management role. And the question was "Do you feel comfortable managing large projects?"

I nailed the response:

"Great question, Lisa. I'll tell you a specific story about a project at Deloitte Consulting. I was the lead Project Manager for a global project. It was a 300-person project, and I was the global PM. It was the most complex project imaginable.

The project spanned seven countries and we had consultants flying in from all over the US. I was tasked with interfacing with two functional leads for the client. It was one of the biggest and one of the most important projects for the client, as well.

In the end, the project was delivered on time and on budget. Don't get me wrong, we had our issues and I still have nightmares about it, but we were able to get it done.

The biggest thing I learned from managing this project is that with so many moving pieces, you can't control everything. My main job as a Project Manager was to make sure different teams were communicating with each other and to manage team dependencies.

I made sure to over-communicate deadlines and their importance. I went out of my way to speak to the leads individually at their desks, during lunch, and before we wrapped up for the day. Communication was key.

I walked away with the confidence that I can manage large projects, should I be asked to do so again."

BOOM! DONE. Notice how I didn't just say, "Yes. I feel comfortable," and talk about how I was Project Manager for eight years. I went straight into the details that I know will not have any follow-up questions. Lisa can't refute what I said.

I use this method to answer almost every interview question.

CHAPTER FIFTEEN

THE SLIMY, GREEDY, UTTERLY NECESSARY
GAME OF SALARY NEGOTIATION

THE BIGGEST PROBLEM WITH MASTERING NEGOTIATION ISN'T that you don't know how to negotiate—it's that you don't have the confidence to negotiate. You either aren't confident or you think negotiation is a slimy, greedy game that you would like to avoid.

I've been screwed out of thousands of dollars many times during my career when it comes to salary negotiation, but in the end it's been the best thing to ever happen to me. That rage inside of me drove me to write this guide with full confidence that it will help others.

I know the old way of doing things doesn't work (here's looking at you, resume). If you want something you've never had, you have to try something you've never tried. No one enjoys negotiating their salary with their current employer, and as I've said, it's easier to just go out and get a new job. But it can be done, as long as you follow my strategy and regain the confidence that's been beaten out of you.

This guide is focused on how to not screw yourself during negotiations, and how to get paid what you deserve. A performance review is not going to reflect what you're actually worth as an asset to the company. If it happens that you end up getting paid more than anyone in your department, then so be it! You deserve what you deserve, and I'm going to do my damn hardest to make sure you get exactly that and not a penny less.

Ready to make some more money? Great, here we go.

Step 1: Know exactly what you want and deserve.

Step 2: The answer to all of your negotiation problems: Leverage.

Step 3: How to master any negotiation, step by step. (Where the rubber hits the road.)

Step 1: Know Exactly What You Want And Deserve.

Confidence can be the difference between a $60,000/year to $75,000/year salary.

The more confidence you have, the better off you are in a negotiation. If you know exactly what you want and what you deserve, the better off you are. I don't mean that you should walk into an office and demand a salary and say: "Take it or leave it."

If you do that, you will crash and burn. Confidence is the ability to define your real value and back it up with evidence and facts. I know this sounds a little far-fetched. Shouldn't the work you've done already speak for itself? Well, that's not how this works.

So, how do you get confidence? It's a two-part process. This works even if you are a pushover, although admittedly it's a little bit more work for pushovers.

First, know exactly why someone would hire you.

I'm not asking you to figure out a couple good reasons why

someone would hire you. I'm asking you to figure out exactly why someone would hire you.

I don't think you should fake it 'til you make it. It's too easy to see past the fake-ness. Evaluating your strengths, what you're better at than anyone else, is a great exercise that will not only aid you in salary negotiations; it will help you keep your interview skills and LinkedIn story fresh and up to date.

No one likes talking about themselves. We would rather discuss other people and their relative strengths and weaknesses. The ability to evaluate and observe yourself in terms of what makes you successful in your industry is crucial to your advancement. Unless, of course, your goal is to plateau, but plateaus are very boring--and financially stagnant--places to be.

This requires a lot of self-awareness. It's right in front of you, but not completely obvious.

Second, know exactly what you're worth, down to the exact penny.

The kiss of death is finding out that someone in a similar role at your company is making a lot more money than you. There is no worse feeling in the world, trust me.

You would feel betrayed, worthless, and eventually angry as hell. Angry that this company screwed you and that you accepted an offer much lower (than others, respectively) mainly because the company told you during negotiations that "this was the maximum they can give you."

Once you find out a coworker is making a larger salary, you realize this is bullshit. But by the time you do, it's already too late; you're locked into this salary. Your negotiation is over, and you were mostly forced into a corner about it.

Do you know how that happened? It happened because you didn't know what you were really worth, and even worse, you didn't know how they really valued you. That gap of information usually ends badly for the job candidate. Remember to always mind the gap.

So how about we avoid this situation? Sounds like a plan. In order to do this, you need to start by negotiating right the first time and making sure you're on the high end of their pay scale.

What everyone else does: They go on salary websites like glassdoor.com and view what other people at the company and similar roles are making. Then they come up with a salary based on that information. I give that approach four out of seven possible points. Sure, it's decent info to have, but it shouldn't be the only activity that you're doing.

These websites tell you what other people are worth, and not what you're worth. Believe it or not, you don't have to get paid exactly what other people get paid.

In fact, who cares about other people? You should get paid the maximum value you are worth to the employer. And so what if that happens to be more than the standard?

Better that you shoot for the moon and land among the stars, than to shoot for the stars and crash into a satellite. No one likes to crash and burn on salary negotiations, regardless of the industry.

So, Robbie – how do I find exactly what I'm worth to employers? There is only one way, and you might not like this option, mainly because it requires work. The single most effective way to understand your worth is to interview and get as many job offers as you can. I call this "exploring your options."

The more you interview, the better you become at speaking with future companies that might have the dream situation you're looking for. The more offers you receive, the more information you have about what your real worth is to employers.

The more information you receive, the more effectively you can negotiate your salary and focus on how you will enhance the value of your new company. Your worth monetarily is connected to what you can accomplish for the company.

If after a slew of offers come in, you still think you deserve more, then the next step is figuring out what the real issue is. Maybe it's a different job in a different industry.

Maybe you're not stressing the value you would bring to an employer. If you're not getting the responses you're looking for, there is a missing element in the process that you've not yet evaluated.

When I was applying for consulting roles, every offer came in between $120,000 and $125,000 a year. And I mean every single damn offer.

It didn't matter how I negotiated it. Now don't get me wrong, this is a great wage to have, but I wanted to break that ceiling. I knew I was worth more, but I wasn't conveying my strengths to the employers properly. I was still viewed as a junior resource.

This realization allowed me to enter into a different phase of my life in which I learned new things, explored different skill sets, and finally smashed that ceiling forever. It took swinging for the fences and not getting the desired result for me to see there was a hole in my approach. Keep track of your results and be honest with yourself.

Step 2: Leverage, The Answer To All Of Your Negotiation Problems

If you don't have leverage in a negotiation, you can throw every single negotiation tactic, tip or trick out the window. Sometimes phrasing doesn't matter. No leverage means you have no negotiation power. Leverage is the difference between making $75,000 a year and making $90,000 a year for the same job.

Here are some examples of leverage:

- You have multiple job offers lined up.
- You were referred to the company by a well-respected Senior Vice President within the company. (This makes it harder for the hiring manager to reject you, since an executive endorsed you.)
- They reached out to you before you'd applied for the job.
- They need to fill the position ASAP, and you don't have any urgency to find a new job.
- You have a rare skillset that they desperately need.

Basically, when you have leverage, you are mentally prepared to ask for a higher salary--AKA a salary that you deserve.

How do you get leverage? You already know how to get it from earlier in this chapter.

Leverage = a strongly defined skillset + a strong network + a well-defined online brand + social proof.

BOOM.

How To Maximize Any Negotiation

Ok, so you have confidence and leverage and now you want to kick some ass during the negotiation? No problem. Here's how.

Maximization Tip #1: Start high and know your ZOPA

(Zone of Possible Agreement). The more information you know about what their upper limit is, the better off you are.

Maximization Tip #2: Negotiate to a better job title, thus increasing your salary by default. You think you've reached the maximum salary limit for your job description? One thing that I've done with great success is to start my interviews by asking about the job title above the one they are interviewing me for.

You have to be careful with this, but in some circumstances it makes perfect sense and works wonders. Let's say the proposed job title is Level 8 Consultant. I would push for a Level 9 Consultant. I did that once and I was able to raise my salary by 35% just by moving up the ladder.

Maximization Tip #3: Avoid negotiation over email as much as possible. Want to make a counter-offer? Get on the phone and say it over the phone. Avoid email like the plague. Several reasons why I recommend this:

You don't want a written record of exactly what you said. It can come back to haunt you, especially if you didn't say something properly.

Your employer has proof of whatever may have gone wrong, and they can bring it up again. At least over the phone, the exact details or wording are not set in stone, because there is no record. This is almost always to your advantage.

Also, the tone of your email can be misconstrued and cause issues. You might seem like a greedy bastard over email, but over phone you can say everything in a much softer way, listing great reasons why you're asking for a new compensation structure.

Maximization Tip #4: You can negotiate more than compensation. Vacation, your work schedule, and your work location are the most common items you can and should negotiate. My only recommendation for this is to really understand what is and isn't possible to negotiate. This can definitely work out with your favor when base compensation is not available.

Maximization Tip #5: When someone tells you "We'll talk about this after you join," assume you'll never get it. You know when someone says, "Well, this is something we can consider in six months?" Sure, that's a great gesture, but my answer usually is "Why not now?"

Too many things change in six months, and they will almost never be in your favor. I know that's cynical, but you should always protect yourself first, because the company certainly is only focused on its own gains. Why shouldn't you be?

Maximization Tip #6: Negotiate with the hiring manager, not the recruiter or Human Resources. I know this isn't always possible, but when given the opportunity, you should push the negotiation conversation to the hiring manager. The recruiter's main job is to get you to accept the offer letter at the lowest fair compensation possible. They aren't trying to screw you, but they're not trying to get you the highest compensation either. They weren't in every single interview and have a limited view of your true value to the company.

The core to negotiation is to understand your value to the company. The hiring manager has a better idea of what your value to the company is than the recruiter, so because of this, you're able to push the limit a little higher than you would otherwise be able to.

The recruiter often has a "max limit" that they can hire you at. They are instructed to not pass that limit unless authorized to by leadership.

By dealing with the hiring manager and leadership directly, you can have an honest and transparent conversation about your value to the company and why you're worth much more than the original offer.

After all's said and done, including you doing your best to prove your value, HR or Recruiting extends you an offer.

STAND STRONG. BE THANKFUL.

You can say "no" and be respectful at the same time. Don't get coerced into anything you don't want to do. If you have a gut feeling something is wrong with the negotiations, walk away and don't look back. Get what you're worth! I cannot emphasize this enough. Know what you deserve and go for it like your future depends on it– because it does. Don't take anything less than what you're worth.

Resources I Recommend

When it comes to negotiation, I read or buy anything that Deepak Malhotra offers. He's a Harvard professor focused on negotiation.

Here are two books by Deepak that I recommend you buy if you want to go deeper into negotiation, not just salary negotiation.

Negotiation Genius

Negotiate the Impossible

SECTION FOUR: THE NON-TRADITIONAL ROUTE

CHAPTER SIXTEEN

ARE YOU A FAILURE IF YOU NEED TO WORK A 9-5?

I WON'T SUGARCOAT THE TRUTH: WORKING FOR YOURSELF leaves you vulnerable to financial curveballs. Look at me. 18 months after I quit my full-time job, I had no choice but to get a salaried job. I called it the "real world." The world I was desperately trying to avoid.

The real world is Plan D. My Plans A, B, and C failed. And most importantly, my cash reserves plummeted. I couldn't make it work financially being an entrepreneur without a stable source of income. Here's how that realization felt:

May 20th, 2013 - New York City

"How much is this luggage?"

"It's $199."

"Oh. What's the cheapest luggage you have? I just need a small handbag. I can't afford this luggage."

"This is the cheapest we have, sir."

Did you ever get to the point where you couldn't look at your bank account because you're afraid of what it was going to tell you? Have you ever added up your expenses in Microsoft Excel and found that you couldn't believe what the total was? I mean, literally not believe that the sum function in Excel was telling you the truth, so you added it by hand?

That was me.

The answer was the same regardless of how I added it up. I was burning $10k/month in expenses, and I had no idea how this happened.

I didn't do drugs. I didn't party. I didn't shop. I didn't travel. I was reasonable with groceries. I had a mortgage and a wife that was more frugal than I was.

How in the world did me "living according to my means" add up to $10k a month in expenses?

My expenses were higher than my income. I was losing money fast. So I flew to New York City to interview for a job I didn't want. This job was my backup plan.

While I was there, the luggage that I've had for a good eight years fell apart two hours before my interview. I was in the middle of New York City and was in a frantic mode to find new luggage. Luggage that I couldn't afford.

I couldn't interview while holding my luggage in complete shambles. I would have been rejected before the first words came out of my mouth. So I made the last-minute decision to buy new luggage. The new luggage that I definitely couldn't afford. I had no choice. I couldn't price-comparison shop. I was running out of time.

I made a choice to not look at my bank account. I didn't want to know the answer if I could afford this luggage or not.

My plan out of this hole was to cash in on Plan D. The one smart thing I did when I quit my full-time job was to prepare for Plan D.

Meaning that if I ever needed to get a full-time job I could make a few phone calls and explore my options. I did this by keeping in touch with previous co-workers. I did this by networking my ass off in Chicago. By taking 250 coffee meetings in 400 days.

I learned new skills every day. Whether it was programming or marketing or writing, I made sure that I was ready to go. "In case of emergency use this hammer to break open the glass." I built my own hammer.

Within a week of deciding that I needed to use my hammer to break the glass, I had three interviews lined up. Everything was going as planned.

All of them were in consulting, even though that was the job I was trying to escape. Nobody saw me as a marketer. Nobody saw me as a writer. Nobody saw me as a programmer. They saw my previous 8 years of experience doing consulting. I was a consultant by their terms. That's what I was good at in their eyes.

I had no time to tell them what my dream job was. Income and stability were what I needed. Fast-forward a month, and all of the interviews were completed. Every meeting went well. I was 100% sure that I would get at least two offers, if not three.

Friday, May 24th, 2013 (Memorial Day Weekend)

I used the leverage of having three solid opportunities to let each company know that they needed to get back to me before Memorial Day. As luck would have it, I got all the answers on the Friday before Memorial Day.

The reality was that my financial situation was in bad shape and I needed income faster than they would ever know.

Then the first phone call came. I took a deep breath while watching my phone ring. "Please let this be good news," I thought to myself.

Rejection #1

"Robbie. I would love to have you on. But, you're a little too premature for what we need here. The team likes you, but let's revisit in six months. We'll have a much better idea of where you fit in at that time."

In a typical situation, this would've been a positive outcome. The company wasn't ready for me, but they liked me. The door was still open.

But not in my situation. Anything that resulted in me not working the following week was a failure.

Rejection #2

"Robbie. We've decided to put the position on hold. The team really likes you, but we need to feel out the market a little bit more. Can we revisit in the next 6-12 months?"

Devastating.

Rejection #3

"Robbie. You're too senior for this position. The team likes you, but unfortunately, it wouldn't be a fit for us. When we have a more senior position open up, we'll let you know."

You know how I mentioned Plan D? This final rejection was Plan Z. I thought I'd had this job in the bag.

And here I was. Jobless. Income-less. Lost. Embarrassed. I secretly wished they just told me that they didn't like me. I wish the company said, "Robbie, you're not qualified for this job." I would have felt better.

It was the longest weekend of my life. I needed to go back and look at my options again. I was determined. The problem? It's Memorial Day Weekend. Everyone is off Monday.

To 99.99% of the world, a holiday on a Monday is a great thing. It meant spending time with family, BBQing, laughing and playing volleyball.

For me, it meant one more day I couldn't apply for jobs. It was one more day I couldn't email my contacts asking for referrals. It was one more day contemplating what my next steps were.

The day I got rejected by three different companies wasn't the longest day of my life. It was that following Monday, Memorial Day. It was the first day I'd felt truly hopeless. I'd thought I had everything under control. I'd planned to make sure this day would never happen. And here I was, in a situation I told myself I would never be in.

Six weeks later I ran into a co-worker at an alumni event. I must have worked with him for less than two days. I'm surprised he recognized me.

He asked me what I was up to and I said: "Just finished my last gig, exploring my options." He was in a hurry, but he said to contact him the next day. He had an opening.

Two weeks later I nailed the interview and got an offer, thus putting an end to Plan D.

The funny thing is that I'm now back to Plan A. Plan A never dies. It just takes a little longer than you want it to.

Many of you know you want out of your 9-5. You know you are more capable than what you're achieving now. Except that you've been in Plan D mode since the day you started your career. Don't let Plan D get in the way of what you want to accomplish. Just keep it there in case your original plan fails.

Plan A all the way.

CHAPTER SEVENTEEN

7 WEEK ENTREPRENEURSHIP PLAN

THE POINT OF THIS CHAPTER IS TO START THINKING ABOUT what your future would look like without a full-time job. I've designed an 7-week course to do just that.

Week 1 Action Plan

Do this exercise in a quiet place.

First, write down *all* of the things you could be doing if you didn't have to work 40 hours a week. Imagine waking up on Monday morning without a full-time job and having enough money in the bank to last you for a while.

You get out of bed, get your coffee...then what? What are you going to do with the rest of your week? Write down what you're picturing and keep it handy.

Next, do these things:

- Get your phone.
- Text five close friends.

- Ask them this question: If you were forced to pay me $1,000, what would you have me do for you?
- When they reply back with something stupid like "strip at my birthday party," reply back that you're really serious. You want to know what they would pay $1,000 for.

Circle any overlap between those two lists—the things you want to do from the first list and the things you'd be paid to do on the second list. Of course, any activity from the first list is still fair game to pursue professionally.

––––––

Week 2 Action Plan

This week is all about doing. You're going to do two things:

1) For each activity that you circled last week, write down a related professional project.

The idea behind this activity is to give you a taste of success and motivate you to continue. Pick one of the projects that you will pursue. Pick one and only one. Do not pick more than one. I want you to focus. You are not Superman.

2) Choose someone who will keep you accountable and make sure that you complete what you listed in Step 1.

Tell that person that you need their help to keep you motivated, and mutually select a date by which time you will have your mini-goal completed.

Create a calendar request that has all the details of what you're going to do and when you'll have the task completed. Make sure to set a reminder that will be sent to you when the date you've chosen approaches.

To give you an idea of what this looks like....

If your goal was to test your dream of opening up a vegetarian restaurant by opening a one-week pop-up restaurant, then your mini-goal would be to create ten recipes that you will have ready on opening night.

You should have each recipe reviewed by five independent, unbiased people with whom you have no affiliation so that you can get proper feedback.

If your goal was to begin freelance marketing, then your mini-goal is to have two paying clients lined up. You will also name your agency, design a basic website and build a social media presence.

If your goal was travel the world and blog about it, then your mini-goal would be to take a two-week backpacking trip to somewhere that you haven't been before. These two weeks should be the first two weeks of your year-long travel plans.

If your goal was to open an art gallery, then your mini-goal would be to launch three small weekend art exhibitions with five artists and twenty art pieces.

If your goal was gain enough passive income that you don't have to rely on a salaried job, then your mini-goal is to make $500 of passive income a month. You might do this by creating a product that fifty people will pay $10 for, or for which five people will pay you $100.

I really want you to think about how you're going to do this. Write it all down and save it. Just keep writing. Write down your theories, your questions, your fears, and what your financial needs would be to accomplish it, etc. Do a brain dump. Get it all out.

Don't worry too much about how you're going to make it happen. Over the next few weeks, I'm going to teach you how to put this into action. I just need you to pick a mini goal and set your mind on the idea that you're going to finish it.

———

Week 3 Action Plan

This week's action plan is to find an association or meet-up in your community that is related to your mini-project and get involved.

If your mini-goal was to create ten recipes for your vegetarian pop-up, then get involved in a food group. If your mini-goal was to take a two-week tour of South America, go to a travel meet-up or South American meet-up.

The content of the event you attend is less important than the types of people you will meet there. You want to find people who will be able to help you achieve your mini-project.

Examples:

- Goal: Open a vegetarian pop-up restaurant
- Mini-goal: Create 10 vegetarian recipes
- Stalk: Local owners / founders / chefs / waiters of every vegetarian restaurant in your area

- Goal: Travel the world for a year
- Mini-goal: 3-week exploration trip to the coast of Spain

- Stalk: Travelers / bloggers who have documented their experiences traveling the coast of Spain

Make a clear list of whom you want to contact and then build as many inroads to that person as possible. Always start at the top.

If you want the chef, then try getting hold of him directly. If you don't know the chef, then start building inroads. They will most likely lead to dead ends, but eventually one will work. The waiter, the hostess, the silent partner in the restaurant, the guy that goes to the restaurant six days a week. The wife / husband of the chef, etc. Build inroads. I can't stress this enough.

It will feel like you are on a wild goose chase, but if you want to make this happen, if you REALLY REALLY want to make this happen, you will take this exercise seriously. It will take time, but with persistence, it will happen.

If your goal is clear, stalking becomes much easier and more productive. I have done this PLENTY of times. Do you know what happens when I finally get hold of the chef, founder, etc.? They tell me, "I appreciate your persistence. Sorry, I've been really busy. I have five minutes. What do you need from me?"

Ah, yes. The million-dollar question. Remember, your goal is to build a long-term relationship with the chef, so be ready to answer this question. Here's what you say: "Chef, thank you so much for taking the time to speak with me. I know you only have five minutes, so I'll make it quick.

#1: I wanted to introduce myself. My name is Robbie Abed and I'm a big fan of your work.

#2: You have inspired me to create my own restaurant. Since I'm new to this area, I am in the process of creating ten recipes that are tailored towards vegans as a mini-project. Here are the names of the ten recipes I'm going to create.

#3: Based on these 10 recipes, are there any recommendations that you'd give me as an aspirational chef / restaurant founder?

The chef's likely, approximate response - "Well, thank you! I'm flattered. Based on my experience, every vegetarian needs a solid gazpacho soup recipe! Here's my recommendation for how to create one.

#4: Thank you so much for your time. Just getting to introduce myself means a lot to me. Do you mind if I follow-up with you in a few months after I create these recipes?

The chef's likely approximate response - "Sure. Tuesday mornings are really the best time for me, since the restaurant is slowest on those days."

#5: Thank you again. Is there anything that I can do for you?

The chef's likely approximate response: "Ummm, not really. Well, actually, we have a special event on Saturday. If you could spread the word, that would be great."

Do you know what your next step is? It's to invite everyone and their mother to this special event on Saturday.

All of your friends are carnivores? Who cares, invite them. They're allergic to vegetables and can die from the smell of spinach? Invite them anyway. I don't care. Your goal is to help out the chef. If a few of your friends die in the process, it will have been worth it.

Warning: DO NOT GO FOR THE KILL IMMEDIATELY. Do not say things like, "Hey Chef! Will you invest in my vegetarian restaurant?" The chef will look at you like you are crazy. Instead, start with relationship-building.

Question: Won't the chef refuse to talk to me because I am going to be a competitor?

Answer: In my experience, the chef doesn't think of you as a competitor. You're a nobody, and pose no real threat. The chef just wants to give back and help an aspiring chef/founder. You don't need to worry about that.

Question: Once I've created a list of people to stalk, where do I start?

Answer: I start with the connections that I meet at the networking events. I ask them directly, "How do you think I should contact this chef? What is he or she like?"

LinkedIn is killer for this. Use LinkedIn as much as you can. The rest is hustle and luck. If your vision is clear, it will happen.

That's all for Week 3. Happy stalking!

———

Week 4 Action Plan

Two things about quitting are generally true:

- If you quit your job to start something new, you will lose a lot of money.
- If you don't quit to start something new, you will lose your sanity.

Let me share a quick, unrelated-but-sort-of-related story.

My in-laws have children that are the spawn of Satan. I have a deal with my wife that we take them out to dinner once a year. It's a lose-lose situation. I lose a lot of money and I lose my sanity in the process.

If I take them out to eat, the kids run around the entire restaurant like they run the place. They'll walk into and out of the kitchen. They also stare at other guests while they're eating their food. They act like it is their own house and their parents don't bother to control them.

It's literally my worst day of the year, every year.

Something needed to change so this year I did something different. I took them to a restaurant where we had a private room. We closed the doors and they ran around like animals, but they couldn't run around the entire restaurant and I didn't have to chase them. We sat down and the buffet was ready immediately. We ate, I paid and we got the f*** out.

I lost a lot of money, but I didn't lose my sanity.

Why am I telling you this story (which I hope none of my in-laws ever read)?

Sanity > money, any day of the week.

Sanity is greater than money, but money creates freedom. Money gives you the ability to take risks you couldn't normally take. Money is a tool to long-term sanity.

Ok, *now* here's your action plan:

Write down three things:

1. The date by which you think you will go insane if your situation doesn't change

2. How much money you will need saved up to quit your job
3. A high-level plan stating how you're going to do it. It should include:

• Where you're going to save money

• Where you're going to make more income (if needed in addition to your paycheck now)

• Things you'll have to do differently

• Things you'll have to continue doing

• How you plan on making money after quitting

Take that list and share it with your close friends, and possibly with your family. The only reason I say possibly with family is because your family might think you're crazy--it depends on the relationship you have with them. Obviously, share it with your spouse or significant other.

Here is a script you can use on your friends:

> *"John, I will go crazy if something doesn't change by December 31st. I need to have <$XXX> saved up for me to make a significant change in my career and life. I wrote down a draft of how I'm going to do it. Can I share it with you? I need your help. I am going to make this happen."*

Your ability to make money is your greatest asset. Don't forget that. It's important to survive and it's important to know how you will continue to make money. Quitting isn't about doing something completely different with the snap of a finger. It's more like one long transitional phase. It might even take three years. That's well within the normal range.

Best of luck!

————

Week 5 Action Plan

First, let me address a question you've probably been asking yourself: What Does This Mini-Project Have To Do With Quitting My Job?

Ah yes, great question. Here's the deal. Quitting your job requires two things:

#1: Having the guts to quit

#2: Knowing what to do and what to expect after you quit

#1 is the easiest. You are one nasty email to the boss away from quitting your job. It's that easy to quit.

#2 is tough. The purpose of the mini-project is for you to figure out what you're going to do after you quit. It's a quick look at what your life will be like and what roadblocks you're likely to face.

I would rather you face them now so you have a better idea of what it's really going to take to quit your job.

Here's what to do this week:

Create a simple survey that gives you informal feedback on your mini-project.

I want you to keep your mini-project moving. I don't like it when things become stagnant. You committed to creating a mini-project, so I'm going to make sure you continue with it. Your survey should do the following:

- Describe what your mini-project is
- Describe why you need feedback
- Ask a minimum of three questions, a maximum of five
- Ask respondents for their email addresses and permission to email them later

The goal of this survey is to get valuable customer insight and information that will help you move your mini-project along.

Here is how to create the kind of survey I'm talking about. You must have a Google account to do this.

1. Go to http://drive.google.com.

2. Click on CREATE -> FORM.

3. Enter the name of your project and click OK. Just choose the default theme. No need to get super fancy.

4. Create the questions and click SEND, which will create the survey link.

5. Share the link! Send via email and/or share on Facebook, Twitter, etc. Your goal is to get *at least* five responses.

6. Do *not* be afraid to ask your friends/followers to fill out the survey. Post multiple times if you have to. Follow up with people who didn't respond. You cannot be passive about this activity.

Now what?

The goal is to use the responses to further refine your idea and your mini-project as well as to get others excited about what you are doing.

Week 6 Action Plan

This is how I used to spend my nights, right before I went to sleep:

Browse internet...scroll...scroll...click on article...meh...back button...scroll...scroll...scroll...click on article...good article...retweet...back button...scroll...scroll...step away from computer...go to bed...open phone...open app...scroll...scroll... click...meh...back button...put down phone...fall asleep.

I woke up every morning and I had no idea what I'd read or even what I'd retweeted the night before. I wasted at least 30 minutes every single night on pointless activity.

I made a pact with myself. If I was going to waste 30 minutes every night, I was going to focus on absorbing content that was generated by people who I believe to be the *absolute best* in their field.

I dedicated every single night to reading content from these three people:

James Altucher (entrepreneur, author, podcaster): He is the only reason I write the way I do. He gave me the confidence to "bleed on the page." I studied everything he did.

Noah Kagan (entrepreneur, ex-Facebook/Mint employee): When Noah speaks at events, he does the questions & answers *before* he begins speaking. He has taught me that success comes from following systems that work. His articles tell you step-by-step how to do things. I buy almost everything he creates.

Ramit Sethi (author of *I Will Teach You To Be Rich*): He has taught me that boring topics can be written in a humorous tone and still be very effective. The tone of my book, *Fire Me I Beg You*, was stolen mainly from Ramit.

Learn from the best and mimic them.

———

Week 7 Action Plan

Have you made any progress? Did you meet anyone new? Did you get feedback about your mini-project?

Here's the deal. This isn't going to happen overnight, over-week or maybe even over-year. *Yes, I just made those words up. They fit perfectly.*

If you've followed my advice in this book then you'll have noticed an incremental improvement each and every day. I know you've heard this before, but if you build the foundation then every step along the way will become easier--I promise.

Step 1: Look at these questions and write your answers down.

Since you've started this program,

1. How many people have told you they loved your project?
2. How many new relationships have you established?
3. How much better off are you today then you were 10 days ago?
4. How much closer are you to meeting your mini-project goals?
5. How many of the past 10 days have you used for achieving your mini-project goals?

Were you really busy over the past seven weeks? You've had seven chances to build your foundation. Are you advancing or are you making excuses?

Step 2: Ask for help.

I'm worried about you. I'm worried that you don't understand that you can't do this alone.

I need you to ask for help.

Call a minimum of two people **that you've met as a result of this course** and ask for help. Tell them that you are struggling and you want their advice.

Here is an email script you can use:

> *Subject: Jenny - Can you help?*
>
> *Hi Jenny - I've reached a roadblock with my career and mini-project. I admire what you've done with your career and it would be great if I could get your insight on how I can take mine to the next level. I'm struggling on what to do with my next steps. Can we set up a phone call? It won't take more than 15 minutes; I promise.*
>
> *In return I'll owe you a favor and I'll help you with anything you need help with. (If you already know what you can help them with, offer that instead.)*
>
> *I know this is a big ask and I would be grateful if you could help. I think you are the right person to help straighten me out.*
>
> *Let me know if next Tuesday xx/xx at 2:00 p.m. works for you.*
>
> *-   Robbie*

This ONLY works if you've met the person and have had an

open dialogue with them before sending the email. You NEED a semi-stranger to tell you the truth. If you don't have a person like this, then please go back and revisit the other weeks and retry those activities. This usually does not work as a cold email.

I call this the midlife crisis call. I did this exact same thing when I was desperately struggling, and the results of the phone calls allowed me to focus on my next steps.

This is a hard email to send, I know. I know you don't want to waste their time. You're not.

I know you're afraid that they might not respond to the email. That's normal. Send the email to give them a chance to not respond.

You need as much help as you can get. You cannot do this alone. People are on planet Earth to help you, not to hurt you. Use them to your advantage.

SECTION FIVE: THE QUITTING PLAYBOOK

CHAPTER EIGHTEEN

READY, SET, QUIT

You've established a network. You've begun interviewing, or you have some interviews lined up, or you're ready to side hustle into your own business. You've stashed away a little (or big) nest egg in the bank. It's time to cut the cord with that dysfunctional, soul-sucking job of yours.

To make this a reality, I need a favor from you.

Due to the nature of this content (i.e. quitting your damn job!), when you read this chapter, I want you to freak out as if you've just robbed a bank and the cops are on to you but don't have any evidence that you're the one who actually robbed the bank. Look both ways when opening the book. Make sure that no one is around.

No one needs to know what your master plans are except you and me. You're going to rob the bank (figuratively, of course)— and no one will have any clue that this was your plan all along.

It'll take one more week to prepare to quit. I have four requests for you this week. I'm going to keep them as simple as possible.

Request #1: Remove your family pictures from your cubicle or office. Take them home with you. Don't pack them all up in one go. Remember, you're Andy from *Shawshank Redemption*. You need to do this in a way that the warden won't notice. If you have a big family start with one picture at a time. Start by removing the kid who has the least earning potential and work your way up.

No one said this couldn't be fun! Always remove your significant other last. I have a newsflash for you: no one really remembers how many kids you have, but they'll always remember your significant other. You need to do this to remove your mental idea of "safeness" from your job.

The more you see pictures of your family at work, the more comfortable you get. The more comfortable you get, the less likely you are to make the leap. You want to quit your job, right? Right??

Request #2: No trash talking to current employees about how unhappy you are with your job. Your new name is Positive Pam. If you are a guy, call yourself Positive Peter; I don't care. Not talking trash is important because I need you to accept the situation you are in. It is what it is. This is your new motto: It is what it is.

Manager messed up another meeting? It is what it is. You received a "meets expectations rating" on your performance review even though you worked 70 hours a week for the past year? It is what it is. Following me yet? Good.

Accept the situation you are in. This is important.

Request #3: Do Not, Under Any Condition, Mention To Anyone That You Are Thinking Of Quitting Or Looking For A New Job.

Want to mess things up? This is how you mess things up. Tell your family, closest of closest friends, people that it's only necessary to tell– and that's about it. Rumors start and move quickly, and you don't want to be that employee who is still working at the company but thinking about leaving. It will start a lot of awkward conversations.

Request #4: Come and leave from work through the back door. No need to make a spectacle every time you walk into the office. Come in and out of the office in the most unnoticeable way possible. Get used to not being noticed. Your goal is to leave this company, so keep a low profile.

All right, you laid the groundwork. Here is exactly what you need to do to leave on a good note:

Step 1: Shut Your Mouth–Tell Only One Person And Let Them Handle The Communication Of Your Exit.

Tell your direct report or a senior colleague that you have decided to leave the company. Do not start telling everyone until you get the all-clear to do so.

What do you tell your coworkers about the fact that you're quitting? You say that you found a better opportunity elsewhere that you couldn't refuse. This is your answer, no matter how much you hate the company or your boss. This is all you need to say. Nothing more, nothing less.

The key here is to let your superior handle the communication. They will trust you more for it.

And oh yeah, do this in person. If quitting in person is not an option, do it over the phone. There is no reason to tell your company you are quitting over email. I don't care if your company invented email. Don't quit over email. I don't care if you've never spoken to your boss on the phone. Don't quit over email.

Step 2: Yes, Two Weeks Notice Is Still Standard.

Three weeks notice is extra nice. Four weeks notice is not recommended unless stated by your contract or an agreement you made with the firm.

Tell your manager the exact date that you're leaving by.

Step 3: Be Appreciative For Once.

I know that whenever I quit a job, I'm usually the happiest person in the building. The fact that you know that you won't have to be part of this shithole again, and others are stuck in it, probably gives you a warm feeling inside.

It's wrong, but it's true.

So do your best to not gloat about what's next for you. Do your job, and get out of there. Show appreciation by being respectful and holding all that glorious gloating inside until you get out of there.

When you're about 300 feet away from the building, you are allowed to scream at the top of your lungs. You deserve it.

Step 4: Lie Like Hell During Your Exit Interviews.

Exit interviews are worthless. Yes, I said it. They are absolutely worthless. Exit interviews are your one last chance to burn a bridge within the company. You know all those nasty things you always wanted to say to people while you worked there, and, well, now is your chance to really let it all out. And you get to do it through a confidential processor--AKA Human Resources.

HR will make it seem like everything you say is confidential, and no one will ever know you said it except him/her. It's true that they don't tell other people *exactly* what you said, but trust me when I tell you that everyone will find out.

Do not turn an exit interview into a consulting session. You will not turn around the company by telling the truth to HR about all the issues within the company. Nothing is changing there. That's why you're leaving–remember?

Lastly, you are not a hero for leaving. You will think you're better because you're on to the next place, but the next place has its own issues! So don't act cocky in the exit interview.

Step 5: Either Send The Best Resignation Letter Of Your Life Or Send A Boring One.

CHAPTER NINETEEN

THE FAMOUS RESIGNATION LETTER

"Do you mind if I send your resignation letter to the entire company?"

This is what the CEO of Deloitte Consulting asked me after receiving my resignation letter.

Two days later he sent my resignation letter to over 10,000 employees.

(From CEO <name redacted>)

Colleagues,

I recently received a message from Robbie Abed, a practitioner in the Technology practice who is leaving to pursue an opportunity in-industry. I was struck by how he captured in his own words our core belief about taking care of our people – especially our focus on mentorship and colleagues for life.

With his permission, I am forwarding this wonderful

illustration of how we actively mentor. Robbie has our best and my thanks go to the colleagues below (and the multitude of others) who brought his mentorship and apprenticeship to life. So in Robbie's own words, here's the reason why this company is special.

Best,

P.S. I made a few small deletions for wider distribution.

From: Abed, Robbie (US – Chicago)

Sent: Thursday, October 14, 2010 5:06 PM

To:<redacted>

Cc: <redacted>

Subject: I won the lottery, bought a million-dollar condo in Miami, and I am retiring at the very early age of 28. This is why I decided to leave the firm.

Well, not exactly. It is true that I am leaving. Tomorrow (Friday) being my last day.

I hate good-bye messages. Well, let me rephrase. I hate the majority of other people's good-bye messages. How could you summarize a great experience with a great company with amazing people in 2-3 sentences? I couldn't do that. I think we all deserve more than a "hey, it's been fun – see you never!"

Through my time here, I have come across some amazing people, many who have directly affected the work I do, who I work for, where I work & when I work. Here are a few people that I can't thank enough (in no particular order):

<name redacted> – Thank you. You helped staff someone you barely knew, on an amazing project even when I threw a

staffing curveball at you last-second. You listened and I appreciate that.

<name redacted> – You were my first career counselor, and along with <name redacted> you directly affected where I was staffed, and it was always for my benefit. Even when you knew you were going to lose me as a counselee you still went out of your way to help me. Thank you.

<name redacted> – Career Counselor #2. You tell it how it is, and that's an amazing thing. You guided me through many difficult situations, spoke the truth and let me make the best decision for myself and <company name> (I'm starting to think I was a difficult counselee!). Thank you.

<multiple names redacted> – I had a great time there, and you guys were the reason I dealt with the delayed flights every week. <name redacted>, sorry I had to beat you so many times in billiards. Some things I just don't lose in, no matter whom I'm playing.

<name redacted> – Thank you for everything. I never knew how bad my writing skills were, until you pointed them out to me! Sorry for recommending the worst restaurants possible in Chicago. I am slowly improving in my recommendation skills. Thank you!

<name redacted> – OK, forget what I said. I'm a horrible restaurant recommender and <name redacted> is always the first to point that out. Thanks for the laughs & putting up with me. I also apologize for you walking across Chicago to find the restaurant I made reservations at. Next time, read directions better, or I'll provide clearer directions. Thank you!

<name redacted>– Thank you for everything. I will miss seeing you front & center in the telesuite calls. Regardless of what

everyone else says, you're the best-looking one in the telesuite. Thank you!

<name redacted> – Thank you for everything. You were always able to guide our team in the right direction, and laugh when the project got stressful. It helps a lot. <name redacted> prepared me for all the writing I was going to do, so hopefully I wasn't too bad!

<name redacted> –Thank you for everything, and I'm sure you will guide the <project name redacted> in the right direction. As with many, you were flexible in my role and let me shine with what I'm good at. I tried to get the new system named <system redacted>, but I guess that doesn't fit in <company name> naming standards. Thank you!

<name redacted>– Career Counselor #3. You're the man. Thanks for being honest with me, and thanks for all of the career advice. Thank you!

I have a local opportunity to do business development and sales for a much smaller company – and I have a feeling that this is what I will be really good at.

I might be back, you never know. I will take full advantage of the alumni program.

OK, Let's dive into it. The science of writing a resignation letter.

You need to send two—yes, two—resignation letters. (P.S. when I say "letters", I really mean emails. You don't need to write a physical letter.)

- The Formal Resignation Letter to HR and your boss
- The Simple Goodbye Email to all your colleagues

Let's start with the formal resignation letter.

The Formal Resignation Letter Template:

The purpose of this is to let HR know your intention to leave the company and when your last day is.

That's it!

Nothing more, nothing less.

It looks like this:

> TO: <*human resources contact*>
>
> CC: <*your boss*>
>
> Subject: *Robbie Abed's Resignation*
>
> *Body:*
>
> *Jennifer,*
>
> *As discussed with Michelle, I am submitting my formal resignation from <company name>. My last day will be <last day>.*
>
> *Please let me know if there are any documents to fill out or any processes that I need to follow before my last day. I really enjoyed my time here and I wish nothing but the best for my co-workers and <company name>.*
>
> *I will send a separate thank-you letter on my last day.*
>
> *Thank you!*
>
> *Robbie*

I highly recommend never putting the reason you are leaving in writing. It *won't* help you and it can, and most likely will, come back to haunt you. To reiterate, I have no issue with you telling your employer why you're leaving. Just don't put it in writing.

A few forwards of that email could end up in the wrong hands... and all of a sudden you're causing unnecessary drama. It is also difficult to process tone over email, and you don't want others making up reasons why you left.

So with regard to a formal resignation letter, that is it. It's really that simple.

You should wait to send your goodbye email until your very last day. The main purpose of the goodbye email is to say to your final farewell and inform anyone that hasn't heard already that you are leaving the company. It's a simple email, but it's often messed up.

Do not offer constructive criticism in your email, or offer suggestions on how to improve the company after you leave. You had your chance to improve it, and now is not the time. You're on your way to bigger and better things.

What you say now needs to be graceful and appreciative and appropriate. The reason the CEO sent my email to the entire company was because I called out co-workers that I enjoyed working with and how they helped me advance my career. I really enjoyed working at this company, and my resignation letter showed it.

Most of all, it was positive and inspiring way to leave the company, even though I could've taken a more negative approach. When I've left other firms, my emails have been two to three sentences at the most, but always still positive and respectful.

I want to emphasize this with annoying periods between each word: Do. Not. Offer. Constructive. Criticism.

Don't offer it in the goodbye email.

Don't offer it in the resignation letter.

Don't even offer it in a private email to your boss or superiors.

Don't even do it in person.

Keep it to yourself.

If you couldn't move the needle while you worked there, what makes you think you're going to help by giving advice after you've already announced you're leaving the company?

There are two goodbye email templates:

- Short And Sweet: Does the job in a professional way.
- Long, Personalized And Thankful: This is the goodbye email that gets you bonus points. An email that none of your co-workers will ever forget.

Let's start with the first template.

Short And Sweet:

All,

If you haven't heard already, tomorrow is my last day at Acme Corporation. I've had a wonderful time here and I'm happy to be part of a great organization.

Just because I'm leaving doesn't mean you can't keep in touch.

<personal email> is my personal email address. Feel free to send me a message at any time and we can connect over coffee. You can also add me on LinkedIn <link to LinkedIn profile>.

This is a bittersweet email for me, and I really want to say thank you again for everything. I've had the pleasure of working with some great people here, and I wish everyone the best of luck.

Thank you again!

Robbie

I recommend sending this email if you had an average experience with the company.

Long, Personalized And Thankful (The Absolute Best Way To Leave):

If you want to quit your job on the best note possible, then this is the resignation goodbye email that you send. This is the format I used before the CEO of Deloitte Consulting decided to forward my email to the entire company.

Not only will you leave on a great note, you will be more loved on your way out than while working at your company. This email is that good. Here we go.

The biggest problem I have with resignation letters is they all say "Thanks for nothing, see you never." Nobody ever says "thank you" and means it.

So that's what you're going to do differently. Instead of saying "It's been fun," you're going to say: "Here are the individuals that made an impact on my career." See the distinction? Then you're going to list everyone who's made an impact on your career. List their full names and tell them how they made a difference in your time at the company.

That's it!

Who do you send this to? There's actually a two-step process:

Step 1: Send to the people you've worked with as you normally would. Always use BCC. You should CC your personal email address, so that when someone replies they can reply directly to your personal email.

Step 2: Forward the email to a few executives and/or the CEO and say the following:

"Don – I'm leaving the company this Friday and below is my resignation email. I thought it would be great for you to see whom I recognized on my way out. Thank you so much for this opportunity. I'm grateful to have been part of an amazing organization."

This is a great way to send a personal thank-you to them even if you haven't worked with them before. I always do this to keep my relationships healthy. Remember that your goal here is to not burn any bridges. In fact, your goal here is to reinforce bridges and make them stronger on your leaving than they ever were during your time there. Odd, I know, but it works.

Step 6: You Aren't Done Yet!

Ah, you thought you could just walk out the door and that's it. No. Keep a strong relationship with your former co-workers. Invite them out to coffee a few months after you leave. Add them on LinkedIn. Keep your connections close.

Nurturing these relationships might be difficult during your final months at the company when you're looking for a job, having to keep your search secret– but there's no reason it should be after you've left. Keep it professional, letting them know what you're up to now and what your future situation is.

Whatever you do, do not use your flown-the-coop-newly-found-freedom to trash talk your old employer with your old coworker, no matter how strong the temptation. They chose to stay, you chose to leave and that's all there is to it. You can still both want to see one another succeed, and be helpful connections for one another without muckraking the employer you had in common.

Also, there's something graceful in letting things go and not re-hashing the wrongs you feel were committed against you at the company. Talk about your future and about how you can help one another succeed in it.

CHAPTER TWENTY

WHATEVER DECISION YOU MAKE, IT WILL BE WRONG

I WAS SCARED TO QUIT MY FIRST JOB. I DIDN'T WANT TO TELL my boss I was leaving. I knew she would be mad at me. I was leaving for a competitor who was also going to pay me more. I was a traitor. How dare I leave a company for better money? She kept telling me that I was making the wrong decision by leaving, and that I shouldn't be making a decision based on how much the new employer was going to pay me.

She was right–I shouldn't have been making my decision to accept a new job based solely on salary. That obviously wasn't the only reason I was leaving, but she was convinced, and for the moment I was relieved.

Did I make the wrong decision by leaving? No, I can safely say I made the right decision. However, if I asked my old boss today whether I made the right decision, she would still tell me no. It wouldn't have mattered if I'd quit and created Facebook and became a billionaire.

In her eyes, I made the wrong decision. It took me a while to realize that every decision I make for myself will always be wrong for at least one person. There will always be someone who is negatively affected by my decisions, even the small ones.

- If you take a job in another state, you will disappoint your hometown friends and family and please the person that hired you.
- If you quit your job, you will disappoint your boss who has to replace you and make the startup community happier because they have a new person in their community.
- If you stay at your job, you will disappoint yourself.
- If everyone agrees with your decision, something is wrong.

When I quit my job to start my own company, everyone thought it was a bad decision. Not one person thought my decision was a good one.

I had a great, steady job with marketable technical skills, and here I was quitting my job and going completely on my own. I was taking a risk, and most people prefer to play it safe and not take any unnecessary risks.

What could be safer than working my life into the ground at a large firm that took care of me? What was the big deal about sacrificing my happiness for long-term security? No one could tell me I was making the right decision but me. I knew what I wanted for myself.

I can safely say I made a great decision. I've reached many of my goals, and I've managed to completely rebuild my business network, which had previously been worthless. I made a great decision. Best decision I've made in a long time.

If you ask my previous employer, they still think it was a wrong one. If you ask my family, they'll tell you they still aren't convinced my decision was right. It's an annoying paradox, but one that happens every day.

You need to make the best decision for your goals, not for what other people want for you. This is your life, not theirs.

How do you know a decision is the right one? You won't know until you've made the decision and lived the results of it. You can "listen to your heart" to figure out if it's the right decision, but I don't even know what that really means so I suggest you ignore that advice.

What if it turns out to be a bad decision? Even better! The next time someone asks you "What's the best mistake you've ever made?" you'll have a story to tell.

There is nothing more interesting than hearing someone talk about a bad decision they made. If that person can laugh at themselves, or cite something that they learned from the experience, even better.

Bad decisions are underrated. Hesitating just fills time with anxiety and regret. Don't fall into indecisiveness. You'll hate yourself for it later.

I will tell you one thing: Quitting takes guts. Quitting forces you to face your fears. You will go through many stages, and probably go through a midlife crisis. You will feel like you've hit rock bottom.

You will start doing things you never thought you would do back when you had a full-time job, and some of these things might be downright embarrassing.

People will doubt you. You will doubt yourself. You will find new friends and acquaintances along the way. Your mother will be worried about you and ask why you don't call as often. You will start looking for a mentor.

You will ask people how to find a mentor. You will Google it and the answers will suck.

You will be lost. You will realize that your vision is a lot different than that of your friends. And then it happens. The day comes that you have it all figured out.

The day someone gives you a compliment that you've never received before. The day you realize you have a skill that you're actually good at! The day that you reconnect with your former boss and for the first time you are 100% confident that you are actually smarter than she is.

The day you receive your first paycheck from a non-traditional source.

The day you tell someone what you are doing with your life and they ask YOU for advice.

The day you go to your family and can't wait for someone to ask you how life is going.

The day you tell someone, "Quitting is the best decision I've ever made."

I know you're worried about quitting. For some of you it's just good ol' fear, but for others among you it is a purely a financial decision. You need every paycheck you get. You live day-to-day with your finances and expenses. You may have a family and responsibilities. You are not alone.

The older you are, the more responsibilities you have, and the harder it becomes to quit. Don't worry. I've been there and was able to get out of it. So will you.

Don't set yourself on fire to make someone else warm.

I've tried telling myself not to care. It doesn't work.

Even when I knew I was supposed to not care. Even after I got a "meets expectations" rating after working every day and night for an entire year.

Even after I was told, "that the policy has changed" so that I was no longer getting a raise I was promised. Even after I got on the wrong side of office politics.

I tried leaving the office early on Fridays so I could get peace of mind. That only lasted one week.

I had been programmed to care, even when it's not in my best interest. I learned, through quitting, to prioritize myself over everyone else.

Today is the day that you do the same. Forget about the mission-critical project at work. Forget about the goals of your boss and company. Forget about what other people will think about you if you quit. Today is the day you stop making everyone else around you warm. You're the one that's cold. Maybe you should start a fire for yourself.

APPENDIX

HOW TO ANSWER THE MOST COMMON
INTERVIEW QUESTIONS

First, let's sort interview questions into two main buckets:

- **Behavioral Questions** – These are the "Tell me about a time when" questions.
- **Everything else** - I like to make things simple. These are common during the first phone interviews with HR.

Let's dive into how to answer behavioral questions.

Behavioral Questions

Anytime the questions start off with, "Can you tell me about a time when?" you know it's a behavioral question. These are often awkward, but they're unavoidable. These are typical examples from my experience:

- Tell me about a time when you didn't get along with a manager. How did you handle it?

- Tell me about a time where you failed at something.
- Tell me about a time when you were in a group that wasn't performing.

So how do you answer these types of questions? The biggest piece of advice I can give is to provide a specific example that you encountered. It is the absolute kiss of death if you start to talk about what you would do. Don't talk about what you would do. Nobody cares. They want to know what you did.

If you find yourself giving a general example, stop yourself and think about other examples.

Pro-tip: have about 4-7 stories prepared in advance that you can easily talk about. Then you can take one these situations and customize it for the interview question.

When answering behavioral questions, I also follow the STAR method religiously:

Situation or Task – Name the particular situation that you encountered. Usually, this situation involves some drama or something going wrong.

Action – What you did to remedy the situation. Not your group member. You.

Result – What was the outcome?

Seems simple enough, right? Here's an example:

Question: Robbie, can you tell me about a time that a project wasn't going well? I'd like to hear more about how you handle stressful situations.

Answer: Great question, Tom!

Situation:

"I was brought in to manage a project that was severely short-staffed and had no clear project deadlines. On top of that, there was a lot of turnover at the client, and this made everything that much harder."

Action:

"The first thing I did was make sure I understood the scope of the project. I heard many different versions of what was supposed to be the project, but no one gave me a straight answer. I put together a presentation of my findings, and I presented it to the executive board. The board then gave me insight on what the real scope was.

I then took that information and came up with a new project and resource plan. We were severely understaffed, so I let the board know that we couldn't complete the scope as intended if we didn't have the right resources. This was an uphill battle, but in the end, I was able to reduce the scope and get a few more functional resources on the team that we desperately needed."

Result:

"The result was we went live with the project on time with the new plan, and without any turnover during the last four months of the project. It was a success, and the project team and board were happy with the results."

BOOM. DONE. Notice how I never said, "Tom, this is how I would handle a project that wasn't going well." It's all about the specifics. You need details or else you will be crushed in the interview. It's obvious if someone is talking from experience or guessing.

P.S. It's a habit of mine to respond with "Great question." It's an ego boost for the interviewer and serves as a good transition to my answer.

———

Can You Tell Me About Yourself?

If there is one question you need have an excellent answer to, it's this one. This question is not: "Can you read off your resume and tell me about every job you've ever had in chronological order?" To succeed at this question, you need to understand why someone would hire you.

My sarcastic answer:

"Hi, my name is George. I'm unemployed, and I live with my parents."

~ George from Seinfeld

Sorry, I had to include that. The goal here is to start off your answer by giving a clear, concise answer as to who you are. If you can't summarize your entire career in one to two sentences, it's not clear enough. I'm not saying your whole answer is one to two sentences, but the first words out of your mouth better be as clear as possible.

"Great question, John. Over the past 10 years, I've had the great pleasure of working for excellent firms such as Accenture and Deloitte as a technical lead and project manager. My strength has always been being a strong tech lead, but also being able to communicate with business executives. This is an area I'm strong in, and would like to continue to working in."

BOOM. There you go. Ten years summarized in one short paragraph. Trust me, I can go down the rabbit hole and give more details, but I want to plant the message as early as possible.

"I can go over my resume if you want, but I don't want to ramble on. Is there anything in particular that you want me to go over in more detail? I'll be more than happy to spend more time discussing it."

Notice how quickly I asked a question of the interviewer? This was intentional, because every interviewer is different. I don't want to waste their time, and I don't want to talk about something that they don't want to hear about in the first place. This is a fantastic way to guide the conversation towards being more productive.

The most common mistake is for candidates to go over everything in chronological order—resulting in a 10-minute, not 1-minute answer. Resist the urge to tell them everything. Trust me; they don't care. It can only hurt you.

Where Do You See Yourself In Five Years?

Why they ask this question: It's simple. Are you a motivated individual or not? They want to hire someone who is thinking ahead because they're interested in your future career path.

My answer: "I'm a big believer in being challenged in my work. I'm always looking to advance my career and at the same time, I want to be happy in my career. I see myself being challenged, and I see myself in a great work environment. An environment that pushes me to become a better person and to learn great skills.

I don't know exactly what title I will have in five years. I'm always looking to advance, but the main thing for me is that I'm learning new skills. I strive to create a good working environment for my colleagues and I hope that others do too!"

Notice how I didn't say things like, "I want to be a manager?" or "be promoted to XYZ position"? I purposely avoid answering with that because we all know it's next to impossible to figure out what's going to happen in five years. I don't know what I'll have for breakfast tomorrow, let alone what's going to happen in five years.

The other consideration is that speculating can cause issues. For example, if you say, "I want to be a manager, like you," then the manager could take that as a signal that you want to replace them. It's far-fetched, but I've learned just to stay away from the specifics. You have no idea what the interviewer is thinking, and you don't want to fall into any traps.

I stick with "advance my career and be happy," and it has worked wonders for me.

———

What Is Your Biggest Weakness?

Why do they ask this question? I'll give you a million dollars if you could figure this one out for me. I know the intention is to find out why they shouldn't hire you, but I'm not sure what answers they are expecting from this answer. However, I do have a firm answer for this question.

> *"Great question. For me, it's all about focusing on the strengths. I think that's where the most value comes from. So, let me rephrase your question slightly. I'll tell you why you shouldn't hire me. You shouldn't hire me if you're looking for someone to just execute sales deals. You shouldn't hire me if you're looking*

for someone to put quotes together. Could I do that? Of course. But I'm also at a point in my career where that's not the best use of my time or yours.

You would hire me because my strength is building relationships with executives and helping them create bigger, better solutions. That's what I've always been good at and that's why you should hire me. I've also been building my network in this industry for the past three years, so I have a head start."

Alternate answer: "Over the course of my time as a business development rep, I've learned a few of my weaknesses and how I've overcome them. Do you mind if share those with you?

The first weakness I uncovered is that I was too lenient with accounts. I would give them too long to make a decision. What ended up happening is that they almost never made decisions, regardless of how much time I gave them. So I learned to be stronger with timelines, and even if I got a firm NO, that would help me move on.

The second weakness is that I wasn't clear on pricing structures. I tried to be lenient with clients on pricing, and in the end, it didn't drive much confidence. I lost a few sales that way. The good news is that my first calls convert to sales at much higher rates than before."

––––––

What Is Your Biggest Strength?

The interviewer wants to know if your strengths are aligned with the strengths needed for the job. It's like a cheat question. Instead of asking questions to determine if you're a fit for the job, they decide to let you determine that for them. Sorry, no more sarcasm from Robbie today.

If you get this question, use your research to tell them exactly what they want to hear. If your strengths don't fit in perfectly with the job description, you don't deserve the job.

Ironically, my answer is the same as for the biggest weakness question: "Great question. For me, it's all about focusing on the strengths. I think that's where the most value comes from. So, let me rephrase your question slightly. I'll tell you why you shouldn't hire me.

You shouldn't hire me if you're looking for someone to just execute sales deals. You shouldn't hire me if you're looking for someone to put quotes together. Could I do that? Of course. But I'm also at a point in my career where that's not the best of my time or yours.

You would hire me because my strength is building relationships with executives and helping them create bigger and better solutions. That's what I've always been good at, and that's why you should hire me. I've also been building my network in this industry for the past three years, so I have a head start."

Why do I answer like this? The quicker I can tell them whether I am a fit or not for the job, the faster the process goes.

———

Why Did You Leave Your Last Job?

I wish "none of your business" was an acceptable answer to this question. However, it is a valid question, and you should have a good answer for it.

There is only one reason why they ask this question. They want to know if you'll have a similar reason for quitting this job. This is a simple, but effective, due diligence question.

For example, if you say, "I quit my last job because they over-worked me," their response might be: "Well, just to let you know, we have a "work hard, play hard" type of culture here. Are you sure you can handle that?" And before you know it, you're on the defensive. You never want to be on the defensive in an interview.

My answer: "I left my job for several reasons, but the main reason is that I had a great opportunity to do something different, and it was something I couldn't pass up. I really appreciated everything my last job did for me, and I learned a lot. It was just time in my career to move on. I still have great relationships from my time at the company, and we catch up for lunch once in a while. I left amicably and gave two weeks advance notice. We both agreed that it was a good move for me."

My answers are always positive, and yours should be too. You know the real reason I left that job? I was sold a bag of bad goods. They told me my job would be like X and it turned out to be a complete lie. I was doing a job I hated. I wasn't learning anything and I did everything in my power to get a new job.

That's the real answer, but I'm smart enough not to say that. As soon as you present a negative vibe, your chances of acing the interview are over.

So, I stick with the traditional "I had a really great opportunity, and it was my time to leave" spiel. It works great and gets them to go to the next question. I also did leave amicably and gave a two weeks notice. I never burn bridges.

———

Do You Have Any Questions For Us?

Yes, are you going to hire me, how much will you pay me, and when can I start?

That's how I would like to answer that question. But, again, if you haven't noticed the theme yet, I stick to the practical, positive answers. Regardless, I always have questions prepared to ask the interviewer.

Why do they ask this question? They ask merely because it's a formality. However, it is obvious they want you to have some questions. Ask no questions, and you'll look like an idiot. It's that simple.

How I answer: First off, I never wait for this question to be asked before I start asking questions. My #1 goal with any interview is for it to be more like an informal conversation. So I ask questions frequently. The better questions you ask, the better off you are.

For instance, I might ask: "First off, thank you so much for this opportunity. I've really enjoyed our conversation. One thing that caught my attention was when you mentioned that an average project length is three months. In my experience, many of the projects I've worked on were at least six months in length. Even the smaller ones were four months long. What makes your projects so different? The reason I ask is I want to understand your delivery process better, and the types of resources needed for your projects."

I'd ask that question first because I genuinely want to know the answer. Secondly, I'm well aware that I am judged by the quality of my questions. I showed that not only am I listening to what my interviewer is saying, I'm also able to ask intelligent questions about why they do the things they do.

The questions I ask are almost always based on something the interviewer's said, and will always prove that I know what I'm talking about. It's why I avoid general questions. I'm going to show that I know my topic inside and out and that I'm able to ask deep questions. If something seems off or different in what they are saying versus my experience, I'll ask them about it directly.

What Is Your Greatest Achievement?

They ask this question because they want to understand what you consider to be a great achievement. They need a benchmark. This question is especially prevalent for managerial or executive positions.

How I answer: "There are a lot of achievements I've had in my career. The one achievement I consider to be the greatest happens to have happened recently. I moved an IT department that was failing in every sense of the word, and I made it a more nimble and customer-focused organization. I brought on a new team and implemented many of the standards that are used today.

The reason it was a big achievement was because there was a lot of resistance internally about making this happen. This type of project had never been done in the company before, so there were concerns about whether or not I could make it happen. I lead the charge on getting executive approval and I managed the project from start to finish. It was a mentally grueling and time-consuming exercise, but we were able to make it happen. The team is in a much better place now. After the transformation was complete, our IT team was able to fix our downtime issues and respond back to IT support tickets three times faster than they were able to before."

Notice that I followed the STAR method to a "T." I gave a very specific, accurate answer, and I mentioned results. I can't recommend enough having a detailed answer ready. We want to hear about your successes.

———

Why Do You Want To Work Here?

Because I like money, and the word on the street is you would pay me more of it than others. Is this true?

I don't really like this question, but it's a necessary evil. Let's be real. If you didn't think the company would pay you more money than you make at your current job, you would never be in the interview in the first place.

Of course, money isn't everything, but c'mon. It's enough to get you to move from one company to another. I like to keep the answer as real as possible while still being politically correct.

#1: "Three reasons I want to work here. The first reason is that my good friend highly recommended this company. I don't take those types of recommendations lightly and I respect his thoughts. That's #1.

#2 – I did a lot of due diligence. I asked former employees and I looked on your website, social media and news. One thing that is apparent is that this company is focused on growth. I'm at the point in my career where I would like to grow, and that is only going to happen at a company that also wants to make investments.

#3 – Culture is important to me. The one thing I've noticed during these interviews is that many of the people I interview with have the same positive attitude. I didn't hear any bad-mouthing or complaining. I'm always focused on the positive, so this was a great thing for me to experience."

I like clear and succinct answers. I usually break it down into a small list of up to three reasons.

Extra tips:

- Don't mention money. Even though that is 95% of the answer. Don't mention it. It won't get you anywhere.
- Don't ramble on. Be succinct.
- Make it genuine. Show them that you did the research.
- Compliment them! Did you notice how every single one of my points I was complimenting them? Make them blush.

In conclusion, with a little preparation, you should be able to walk into an interview with no more nervousness than you'd feel before trying a slightly spicy pepper.

In other words, with proper research, you can answer these questions very powerfully every time. Remember to spend a significant amount of time coming up with different stories from your career that you can use during these interviews.

CASE STUDIES

In the following section you'll find a few examples of what quitting looks like in real life, along with the exact steps each person took to take it to the next level. You can find more case studies when you sign up for my email list on FireMeIBegYou.com

———

How Jason Went From $83k To $200k In Two Years

Jason was a salesperson for a growing company in a booming hot industry. He was also a classic overachiever, which is not necessarily a bad thing. The problem was that he was making his company millions of dollars and he was making less than 4% of the revenue he brought in! He wasn't being compensated by his company for all that overachievement.

He did what everyone does when they want a raise. He looked on websites that tell you how much he should be getting paid for his position. He did other market research. He was prepared to lay out all the facts.

The evidence was overwhelming, and he came in presenting cold hard facts: he was severely underpaid. He gathered up all of this evidence in a nice folder, set up a meeting with his boss, and went over every single document. The result?

Rejection. They had no budget, and according to HR, he was being paid market value.

What do you do when you run out of options? You call Robbie! Notice a trend yet?

Six weeks later he was making $7,000 more. ($83,000 to $90,000)

Six months later he was making an additional $30,000 more. ($90,000 to $120,000)

Two years later he was making $80,000 more for a competitor. ($120,000 to $200,000)

That's a 240% increase, for those counting at home.

> *"I was always a top performer. I was passionate about my job. I worked my ass off day in and day out. I just wasn't getting paid enough. I tried every trick in the book to negotiate my salary, but I always got the same answer: "We don't have the budget."*
>
> *I followed Robbie's techniques, and within six months I was making $37,000 more. I thought that my employer would hate me for negotiating, and it turns out after my negotiation they respected me a lot more. It was from that moment on I realized how valuable I was to this company and I make sure I GET PAID :)."*

The good news for you is I'm going to share with you exactly how he did it.

Step 1: He threw his salary market research in the trash.

Jason spent six hours doing all the research, collecting evidence, and laid out a factual case. All his hard work resulted in was a big fat NO. He needed another plan.

Step 2: After an initial rejection, he asked that the company reimburse him for half of his rent on his apartment, about $600 a month.

"I was traveling all the time. After they said no, I said the least you can do is help me pay for half of my apartment, since I never really get to enjoy it."

They agreed and reimbursed him $600 a month—which turned out to be a $7,200 yearly raise! This was easier for them because compensation had to get a separate approval, which they "didn't have the budget for."

Step 3: He called an ex –colleague with whom he had maintained a strong relationship, asking for advice.

Jason was still not getting the pay he thought he deserved. He was determined to leave at this point.

This is where most people would update their resume, go on career websites and start applying for open positions. He knew his time would be wasted with that. He didn't want to get through the entire interview process only to realize that he wouldn't be paid as much as he wanted to be.

He sent one email to an ex-colleague that left to a competitor years before. This ex-colleague gave a strong referral to his current employer. Jason went through the interview process and was offered $120,000 total package! A $30,000 increase from what he was making.

Step 4: He went back to his current employer with one simple demand. "Match my new offer or I'm leaving!"

There was only problem. He didn't want to work at this new company, but was prepared to leave in case his current employer didn't match.

"I had an offer in hand, and I wanted to tell my current employer to match it, but I really didn't know how. I knew if I told HR they would have laughed at me.

I didn't go to HR; I went to the person who had the highest vested interest in keeping me. In this case, it was the Senior VP of the company, with whom I had a great relationship. This is what I told him in person:

"John, I really enjoy working here. As you know, I haven't been happy with my compensation. I want to let you know that I have another offer on the table for total compensation of $120,000. I want to stay here, but the gap between my current pay and this offer is too much. If you match it, I will stay. If you don't, unfortunately I will have to leave.

You are the only one within this company to know. I'll keep my mouth shut but I would appreciate it if I can work directly with you on this ask."

He knew the Senior VP would be directly affected by his leaving. The great news was he was on board and supported Jason. Jason had an internal champion!

Through several conversations, HR came back to him and said they'd match the job offer only if he could provide physical proof. He agreed as long as he could disguise what company the offer was from.

They agreed. He brought the offer letter. They matched it.

Step 5: Send a "thanks, but no thanks" offer to prospective employer.

He didn't want to burn a bridge with the employer's offer. Here are some things he did really well.

1. He offered a different way to get paid (reimbursement for half his rent) when he was presented with an initial answer of "no" regarding a pay raise.
2. He never accepted the new company's offer. He received the offer letter and said he needed to consider it in more detail. He knew that if he accepted it and then told them he wouldn't join, that would be a very unprofessional move. Remember, he was READY to leave if his current employer didn't match.
3. He told his current employer the truth and backed it up with the real offer letter.
4. He hid the identity of the company. Never under *any* circumstances reveal with whom you are talking *unless* the deal is signed. This could put you at risk at both companies. This was a very close industry, and all it took was one phone call to see what was happening and he would be in a sticky situation.

Step 6: Find a new job one year later.

Even at $120k total compensation, Jason wasn't convinced he

had reached his maximum number. He also knew that he couldn't negotiate any further with his current company.

He went on his job search and again, instead of looking for job applications, he kept in touch with ex-colleagues who now worked at competitors.

He reached out to them and had informal conversations about opportunities. He had casual conversations with VPs of those companies about how they were growing.

Five weeks later he had a new job offer on the table from a VP of a competitor.

Step 7: He negotiated like a pro.

HR asked him for his pay stubs at his previous company. Jason politely declined.

He told them verbatim, "I'm looking to get paid what my value is for this role. I think it's better to discuss what others at my job level within this company make. I'm not sure if my current compensation is relevant to the discussion."

(Jason knew that if he gave HR his pay stubs, his new offer would be impacted by what he currently makes. Since he was under-paid, it was in his best interests to decline what they were asking for.)

HR persisted for the pay stubs, but through conversations with the new hiring manager, he was able to get HR to back off the demand and provide a new offer without this information.

The new offer was for $195,000 a year. This was a $75,000 increase from what he was currently making!

Jason knew better than to take the first offer, so he came with a counter-offer. He now makes $200,000 a year + commission + equity. He averages $300,000 a year.

Lessons Learned

1. The easiest way to get a new job is through a referral from a colleague you used to work with.
2. Facts and market research generally don't work when it comes to raising your compensation.
3. Getting another offer is the easiest way to get what you're worth. However, you must be prepared to leave if your company doesn't match the offer.
4. To significantly raise your salary, you must have another job offer for leverage.
5. Don't be a pushover during negotiation. Just because they ask for it doesn't mean you have to say yes to it.
6. If at all possible, don't reveal your current salary.
7. You need an internal champion to apply pressure to HR when negotiating pay.
8. Go out of your way to keep in touch with colleagues you have lost contact with.

———

How I Increased My Salary By $25,000 With One 15-Minute Phone Call

HR: Robbie, we are extending an offer to you of $125,000 with a $5,000 bonus and your start date is June 4th.

Robbie: Thank you so much. What level is this for?

HR: Level 7.

Robbie: slight pause.... Thank you so much for the opportunity, I really appreciate it. I'm afraid that this offer is a good start, but it is much less than I'm expecting. For me to come on, I would really need for my salary to be at least $155,000 and with a $10,000 bonus.

Also, from my research, it seems that there is a Level 8? I spoke with a few people at your company and I strongly believe I need to be at Level 8. I've been performing at this level for the past two years now and Level 7 would really be a downgrade for me.

If you need any additional support to get me to Level 8, please speak with Lisa, who is a partner within your firm. She can support it. I've been in touch with her throughout the process and so she is aware of the situation.

I'm extremely confident that I can perform well at this level.

HR: Well...sigh...I'll have to go back and go through a special process. I will say that level 8s are only given to internal candidates. I'll let you know, though.

One week later...

HR: Great news, Robbie! We're able to get you approved to level 8 and bump your salary to $150,000 and $8,000 bonus.

I start the new job, and within a week, a coworker pulls me to the side and asks to talk privately.

"You have seven years less job experience than I do working for similar companies. How are you at level 8 when they've been telling me I won't be able to get level 8 for a few more years? How did you do it?"

The answer is simple.

I had leverage. I created a situation in which HR had no choice but to offer me the job on my terms.

Here's how I did it:

Step 1: I got a referral.

I found out about the opportunity through an alumni networking event that a former employer hosts twice a year. As I was walking out, I run into a former colleague. He asked what I'm doing and I said:

"Independent consulting focusing on leading technology teams as a project manager."

His eyes light up and he goes, "Perfect! I have a great opportunity for you. I'll send you an email tomorrow morning."

> **PRO-TIP #1:** Only go to strategic networking events. The rest are a waste of time. I only go to a few networking events a year. I make sure to attend this one every time for this exact reason. The people who come to these events all share something great in common. We all want to help each other out, since we've all worked with each other at the same company. I knew I would maximize my chances of finding something at this event.

> **PRO-TIP #2:** Know how to answer the question "So what are you up to?" See how clear my answer was? This immediately triggered an opportunity that he was looking to fill. I didn't say anything besides that.

Step 2: I called a partner I used to work with who's at the prospective employer's company.

I talked to her about the position, the levels and the salary. She gave me all the inside information about what to expect in terms of hiring levels and compensation.

PRO-TIP #3: Have coffee meetings with former colleagues. I hadn't worked with this partner in over six years, but I always keep up with her and said hello over email. We have coffee whenever she is in Chicago. I kept this relationship warm because I knew we would need each other later.

PRO-TIP #4: Use your connections to get inside salary and job information. I didn't have to look on the salary websites to see what the pay was! I had an inside connection who told me everything. That's how I knew I could get away with becoming a level 8. I didn't give them "market rates" for the position based on data on Glassdoor. I knew that wasn't going to work because they already knew what the market rate was!

PRO-TIP #5: Push for the better title during negotiation. I knew that they couldn't raise my compensation above $125,000 if I remained at Level 7. So instead of just asking for a pay raise, I ALSO asked to be Level 8 all because I knew that was the only way this was going to happen. Asking for a level upgrade is the easiest way to get a compensation increase. I actually didn't care if I was a Level 8 or not. The role was still the same.

Step 3: I knocked the client interview out of the park.

The opportunity was for a consulting gig directly with a client, so I had to interview with that client first. She asked me:

- "Where do you see yourself in five years?"
- "Tell me about your background."
- "How do you handle difficult projects?"

I had specific and powerful answers for each of those questions. That's all she needed to hear. Within 10 minutes of the interview, I was actually interviewing her. I flipped the script. It was my evil plan all along. :)

Step 4: I used my inside information and my connection as leverage during the negotiation.

"Don't believe I'm a level 8? Ask a senior partner. She will tell you that I qualify for it. You can also refer to the client interview. It went really well." That was all I really needed to say. Remember, I was already referred in through my connection at the alumni networking event. This was just the icing on the cake.

One 15-minute call could mean the difference between $125,000 a year and $150,000 a year. Are you sure you're getting paid what you're worth?

_____

"Why do you need a raise? Doesn't your boyfriend have a good job?"

That's what Christine's boss told her when she asked for a raise during her annual performance review. Here are the exact steps she has taken to go through several career breakthroughs in under six months.

Her dream was to work for a large publishing company.

She had one big problem: She had zero connections in that industry. She had a limited budget and was 1,500 miles away from New York, where all the publishing jobs she was looking at were. Quitting and taking a road trip to NYC without anything lined up was absolutely out of the question. She needed to have a solid, comprehensive plan.

Before: Dysfunctional employer, not doing what she's capable of, wants to be in New York City, has zero connections.

Two months after using my techniques: Lives in New York City, works for a major academic journal, has two side freelance jobs, part of an elite publishing program, and has broken down the barrier to the publishing community.

She did all of this *before* quitting and *before* moving to NYC.

Step 1: She updated her LinkedIn profile.

Her LinkedIn profile was confusing. It said a lot, but it also said nothing at the same time. She used buzzwords like "team player," "results oriented," and "excellent communicator." She talked about herself in the third person.

To put it bluntly, her story sucked! It represented where she was, not where she wanted to be. She made a few significant changes right away:

1. Explicitly stated her value statement as the first sentence.
2. Told a fantastic story of why she loves editing.
3. Blocked her colleagues from LinkedIn so they couldn't see her new profile and wouldn't get any ideas that she was starting to look for a new job.
4. Turned off the setting in LinkedIn that alerted her connections while she worked on updating her profile.

Once this was complete, it set the foundation for her to start reaching out to connections confidently knowing her online brand was a replica of her offline brand. She wasn't leaving anything up to chance.

Step 2: She used LinkedIn to amplify her brand.

LinkedIn publishing is an AMAZING tool to get your word out. Christine wrote an article about her experience called "7 Ways to Find Your Voice." It was her first post and it accumulated over 1,000 views, 83 likes and 18 comments! WHOA.

I'm not kidding when I say it took me over a year to get anything close to those numbers on my blog. She did it on her first try.

This was a shock to Christine because she had never published an article like this. She was always a "behind the scenes" person. The people that commented were others in her network, plus others who'd simply enjoyed her article--and who requested to connect with her on LinkedIn. A sample of some of the titles those commenters held:

- International Abstract Artist and Published Author
- Marketing and Public Relations Director
- Senior Program and Curriculum Coordinator

These were all people that had jobs that she wanted, or were in senior positions at companies that could potentially use her help.

What you need to know:

- You don't need a huge following to see these types of results. That's the benefit of using LinkedIn publishing.
- Telling a story *always* gets more shares than doling out generic advice.

- After writing an article, take a look at who commented, liked or shared your article. Find out who would be the most interesting for you to talk to, and reach out to them directly. Since *they* shared *your* article, it's not as creepy as it sounds to reach out to them. You built something of value. They liked it. If you see fit, you can now build strong connections with people that can help you find your next job.

Step 3: She asked the right person for help over coffee.

Prior to her move, she wanted to lock down an editing job for a publisher in New York. She didn't know where to start. The publishing industry is almost impossible to break into if you don't know the right people. She also didn't want to apply for jobs online because she hadn't had any luck with that process.

I asked her one simple question: "Who likes you the most, and is doing something similar to what you want to be doing?"

It turns out a professor from college loves her work. They sometimes kept in touch, but not often. Christine wanted to reach out to him, but felt weird because she had not talked to him in a long time. She didn't want him to feel that she was using him.

She invited him for coffee via email. The email was five sentences long. He was happy to hear from her and agreed to meet up for coffee.

She told him that she was thinking about quitting her job and very clearly told her professor what her new value statement is and with whom she needed to be in touch with in NYC.

That's all he needed to hear. Two months later, she was the managing editor for a journal based in New York City--where she wanted to be. Her professor made a few phone calls and several coffee meetings later with those contacts, she secured a position. All because she asked him for coffee and told him *exactly* what she was looking for.

And to think she was hesitant to ask him for coffee just because she didn't know how to frame the original email.

What you need to know:

- Coffee meetings are a *fantastic* and *effective* way to uncover job opportunities.
- You must have a *clear* and *simple* value statement so others know how they can help you. It should be one to two sentences long, maximum.
- Coffee meetings can be a waste of time, but not if you set them up properly.
- Being clear in your ask about who you need to get in contact with will significantly increase your chances of success.

Step 4: Get connected to the Super Connectors in the publishing industry.

Do you know how many emails it took Christine to get on a phone call with someone five times more successful than her in her dream industry? One email. The email was four sentences long.

It took me four years to get a hold of James Altucher. It took her one four-sentence email.

One week later, she was on the phone interviewing someone she thought would never respond to her email, let alone agree to spend a half hour on the phone with her and give her free advice.

Do you know the best part about all of this? The person she interviewed now owes her a favor! Christine helped her get publicity and helped bring brand awareness to her business. Isn't that crazy?

Christine is going to nourish this contact and utilize it when the right situation arises.

This was her email to me: "You are literally the world's greatest. Thank you!!! I can't believe this is real life. That was my very first super connector email!! I didn't even expect a response. Now on to interview questions!!!"

What you need to know:

- All successful people check their email.
- It is SUPER EASY to get their email addresses.
- Everyone is Googling you. So when you send these cold messages, it's important that your LinkedIn profile is not only up to date, but tells an amazing story.
- PRO-TIP - Google yourself right now and see what comes up.

Summary

I'll let Christine summarize:

> "Honestly, I counted the months from when I started your program and it only took me one month from when I started to lock down two freelance jobs, two months to sign on as managing editor of the academic journal, four months to lock down a new job–and actually six months to have my entire move/transition planned and completed.

That is a pretty legit timetable. I would have never believed it could happen so quickly when I first started."

———

How Melodie Negotiated November and December Off

Let me introduce you to Melodie, who has the dream situation. Here is an email she sent me recently.

> *"I'm directly compensated for my time (and make more per hour), I am less invested in the bullshit, I have more flexibility, I'm taking November and December off, and they still love me."*

That last line is my favorite. November to December!

By the way, she only works Monday through Thursday, with three days worked from home. The best part is even with two months off, she still makes as much as she did at her previous job.

I don't believe in dream jobs. I do believe in jobs that you can do on your own terms. You have a 0% chance of creating success on your own terms when you start by applying for jobs online without the right relationships.

I'll let her tell you how she pulled this off. Take it from here, Melodie!

Here is how I did it:

Step 1: I changed how others thought about me.

For nine years I was a Change Management Consultant for the same consulting company. It was time for a change (no pun intended), but I didn't know where to start to change my stigma.

I wasn't sure what I really wanted to do next. I had some ideas, but for nine years my name was associated with Change Management.

I started with my LinkedIn profile and updated it to represent the true me. I stopped treating my LinkedIn profile like it was my resume. I knew everyone was going to Google me, and since LinkedIn showed up on top of Google for my name, I knew I had to change it.

I stopped thinking along the lines of "This is what I did with regard to my change management career," but "This is what I'm truly capable of."

Step 2: I stopped filling out job applications.

If I wanted to get back into Change Management Consulting, then maybe I would have considered using this, but since I wanted a job slightly different than my main experience, this would hopeless for me.

None of my professional job experience would match the keyword matching that the job searching needed. I also had no interest in filling out large forms just for me to get rejected. I've been down that road before, no thank you.

Step 3: I had coffee meetings with connections I hadn't spoken to in a while.

I know Robbie is the expert at this, so I stole this directly from him. Here is who I reached out to:

1. Ex-colleagues who still work at my previous company
2. Ex-colleagues who moved on to different companies
3. Alumni of my college

I found that these people were the most willing to meet with me. The response was actually amazing.

During these coffee meetings I was finding out opportunities that I had no idea existed. Although none of the opportunities panned out, I realized how big the "hidden job market" really is. Every coffee meeting gave me more information about how I should be focusing my job search, along with a lot of "insider information."

Step 4: I reached out to the super connectors in Chicago.

I knew I was missing out on a big professional network in Chicago because I spent so much time doing my job and not focusing on building relationships with people who could connect me.

This was more difficult than reaching out to people I didn't know. I could reach out to former co-workers and ask for coffee and I really didn't need a reason besides "let's catch up."

The super connectors were the problem. I didn't have access to them, so I needed a reason to meet with them. A real great reason.

I used a technique straight out of Robbie's handbook.

I asked to interview them. You can see the results of my hard work on belikepeter.com. I did this without any technical knowledge beforehand. I learned a few new tricks and found out how easy it was really to maintain a blog.

Step 5: I always started from the top.

I was actually afraid to reach out to people. I didn't want to bother them because they were busy. Using the coffee and super connector techniques, my response rates were a lot better than I expected. People were HAPPY to speak with me.

I now know how to reach out to anybody and as long as I frame the email properly, I don't have anything to fear. I used these techniques to reach out to extremely busy people and had a lot of great success.

Step 6: I "got lucky" and got a long-term contract offer from someone I used to work with.

Finally, I got the phone call I was looking for: "Melodie, I'm looking for someone to fill a role internally on contract. Your name keeps coming up. Are you available to work?"

This is the best part. I worked with this person for three years. I kept in touch with her for a year after I quit. We had coffee meetings and exchanged emails. My relationship-building effort worked perfectly

It also helped that when I resigned, I left on a great note.

She also saw me as very active on social media and was keeping in touch with my progress. I was at the top of her mind at all times.

The best part is that I didn't have to prove myself during the interviews. Since I came highly recommended from the hiring manager, the interviews were simply conversations.

Step 7: I got the "inside information" on what working in this department would be like. I also got salary intelligence from a reliable source.

I'd already left a job and joined a company I hated two months later. I didn't want to make that same mistake again.

Using LinkedIn, I was able to find the right people I should reach out to. I wasn't connected to them directly, but I did have connections in common with them. I used Robbie's techniques to get a proper referral to them where we had a coffee meeting.

I couldn't believe how much information I gathered in such a short time. They were all open and willing to help me.

Step 8: I negotiated and actually got what I wanted!

One week later I got the offer with the compensation that I wanted. Even though I'd worked with this person before, it was kind of unnerving negotiating with her. I didn't want to come off as greedy.

However, that wasn't the case and she appreciated my negotiation.

Because it's a large company, I was negotiating to HR, but I used my strong inside connection, who was able to place pressure on HR to get the compensation I was looking for.

Step 9: I negotiated again when my contract was up for renewal.

I knocked the contract out of the park. They really wanted to bring me on. I said, "Sure, I would love to join. Here's the thing. I'm taking off November and December. I know this is a busy month for our teams, but this is something that I've been planning for a while."

I was floored when she came back and said "OK. That's fine. As long as you do some extra work in October to make up for the work you're missing in November and December."

I said "SURE THING!"

The kicker is that I get paid for that extra work since I'm an independent consultant.

I know this sounds too good to be true, but these changes are possible if you stop being a pushover during negotiations.

———

HOW HASHIM BEAT THE SYSTEM TO GET A JOB AT HIS DREAM COMPANY

I'm going to let Hashim talk about how a simple employee referral got him a job at his dream company even when he didn't meet the minimum requirements. Read on:

I was a senior in college with a few internships under my belt. I had my eyes on working for a large consulting company, but there was a big problem.

My GPA didn't meet their standards for new graduates for the program I was applying to.

They required a 3.2 GPA. I had a 3.1 GPA. This company is very strict when it comes to these rules.

I applied online anyway, but got rejected pretty quickly through their system. So, what does someone do when they run out of options? They call Robbie.

I knew Robbie worked there, so I reached out to him looking for tips. He stressed how important it was to get a referral from within the company. I sent him my resume + the job posting URL.

Robbie forwarded my email to someone he knows who works at this company. It wasn't a senior contact, but it was better than anyone that I knew.

Robbie's contact submitted my resume to the job posting internally. One week later, I got a phone call from HR for an interview. Two weeks later I was interviewing on site for the job. They tell me it's between me and another candidate.

One week later, I received a job offer.

At this point, I was pretty floored, because I initially didn't "qualify" for the job, and now I work at one of my dream companies. I also beat out the other candidate, but was unsure of why I was more qualified than them.

Fast-forward to my new-hire orientation: All the new hires got to know each other, and during conversation, we come to the subject of how we all got our jobs.

I found out that of the ten new hires, eight of them were from internal referrals.

I found out that the other two were military personnel under a special program. Not a single person I met during orientation received a job offer through the normal application process.

Fast-forward to a company event six months later: I meet the HR person who interviewed me and prepped me for the other interviews. I asked her one simple question: "I'm curious. You told me that I was against another candidate. Why did you choose me over the other candidate?"

She said to me, "It actually was a tie. You were both qualified. However, since you came in through an internal referral, you won. We have done a lot of research in this area, and it's been proven that candidates that are referred internally end up staying in the company longer and are generally better performers."

WOW.

I think it's important to note one thing. I never met or spoke to the person who actually referred me. All I know is that Robbie knew him. The person who referred me was actually in the UK, has no relation to my job, and didn't know anyone in my division.

I guess it didn't matter where it came from or who it came from, as long as it was internal referral. The good news for the person who referred me is that he got a cash referral bonus.

Here is what you need to know:

1. Referrals matter, and are serious business to employers. With every job application, you should be utilizing your connections to talk to whichever person can help you get the job.
2. You don't need to know the person working at your target company! You can utilize your second-degree connections (hello, advanced search on LinkedIn!). No more "I don't know anyone who works for that company" excuses!
3. People get paid to refer others that get hired. My contact got paid over $3,000 for simply submitting an internal referral. It was triple-win situation. Hashim got a job. My connection got paid. I get good karma, and Hashim owes me a big favor. So if you're ever feeling guilty for asking people for referrals, just know they most likely get paid by their company to refer you.

ACKNOWLEDGMENTS

I want to thank James Altucher for agreeing to write the fore-word. James had a profound impact on my writing career, and it's a dream come true that he even agreed to write this. Thank You.

I also want to thank my editor Leah Trouwborst for helping me put this all together, Nate St. Pierre for helping with the final edits, Tim Klein for my back cover photo, and Andrej Semnic for designing the cover of the book.

BUT WAIT — THERE'S MORE!

FIRST OFF, THANK YOU FOR TAKING THE TIME TO READ AND finish this book.

As an expression of my gratitude -- and to follow my own advice, I want to offer you something in return.

I created a program that covers how to build relationships with influencers and executives to help you land a great job without having to apply for it online.

Go to FireMeIBegYou.com to get free tips on how to land a great job without ever filling out a job application.

Made in the USA
Middletown, DE
21 August 2019